GLYNIS HAS YOUR NUMBER

GLYNIS HAS YOUR NUMBER

*Discover What Life Has in Store for You
Through the Power of Numerology!*

G L Y N I S   M c C A N T S

NEW YORK

Library of Congress Cataloging-in-Publication Data

McCants, Glynis
    Glynis has your number : discover what life has in store for you through the power of numerology! / Glynis McCants.—1st ed.
        p.   cm.
    Includes bibliographical references (p.   ).
    ISBN 978-1-4013-0142-2
    1. Numerology.   I. Title.

BF1729.N85M33   2005
133.3'35—dc22

2004054073

FIRST EDITION

20   19   18   17   16   15   14   13

THIS LABEL APPLIES TO TEXT STOCK

I want to dedicate this book to my mother, Gwen McCants. I have often thought that I am so lucky to call her Mom, but I would be honored just to know her. I have never met any woman in my life who has such a huge capacity to love so many people. Her love for her eleven children and their offspring is completely unconditional. Yet her love for the students she teaches art and English to is just as strong. I am also grateful to her for all the help she gave me in writing this new edition of *Glynis Has Your Number*. Thank you, Mother, and may God bless you always.

I also want to dedicate this book to Lynn Aase. As my schoolteacher and mentor, he taught me that with focus and determination, there was nothing I couldn't achieve. I thank you, Mr. Aase, for the profound impact that you have had on my life.

———————

Acknowledgments

I want to acknowledge Kathy Giaconia, who first recognized the importance of my gift with Numerology, and as a producer, came up with an idea that would first get me on *The Leeza Show*. She then went on to produce five one-hour specials with me as the only guest and blew me away with her remarkable producing skills. Kathy, your brilliant mind and clever ideas make you the perfect 5 Life Path. You are a consummate professional and I thank you.

I want to thank Leeza Gibbons, who in my opinion is one of the sincerest people I have ever met in show business. You are a fantastic interviewer and a great pleasure to work with.

I want to acknowledge Charlie St.Denny Youngblood. I really did manifest you into my life by using Numerology, and I have never felt such *unconditional love and support*. I love you, Charlie, and I thank you.

Contents

～

GLYNIS HAS YOUR NUMBER

One

Introduction to Numerology

The true spirit of delight, the exaltation, the sense of being more than man, which is the touchstone of the highest excellence, is to be found in mathematics as surely as poetry.

—BERTRAND RUSSELL (1872–1970)

If you are reading this book, you are turning to Numerology in an effort to improve your life. Like most of us, you are seeking peace and serenity.

I have good news for you—you've come to the right place. Numerology will free you from the bonds of your past, and help you take an active role in determining your future. It answers the questions: What am I here to achieve? What will make me happy? What are my natural gifts?

After doing Numerology for nineteen years and having done well over 9,000 readings, I know you can do effective emotional and physical healing in your life by the numbers. Each time I break down the numbers, a story unfolds. I can look at my client's chart and instantly see the origin of the conflicts in their life. I tell them their strengths and their weaknesses, and show them how these characteristics interact to produce joy and pain—and what the client can do to improve their own experiences. That's why Numerology is so healing. It helps you recognize what you really want; it can help you find your way to success. The purpose of this book is to help you know yourself. What is your Life

Path Number? Soul Number? Personality Number? Power Name Number? Birth Day Number? And finally, what is your Destiny Number? Understanding what these numbers mean will give you the information needed to bring out your greatest good, and give you the understanding to avoid unnecessary conflict with others. I named this book *Glynis Has Your Number* because although the Pythagorean Number System is the one that I use, I also give you my own personal conclusions. I have had many breakthroughs in the science that I'm passing on to you. My insights are sprinkled throughout this book in the hopes of making Numerology extremely easy for you to apply when looking at your personal life. Simplifying the Science of Numerology for everyday use makes this the ultimate self-help book.

▪ PYTHAGORAS AND THE BIRTH OF NUMEROLOGY ▪

Numerology is not new, and it's not a fad. Since the dawn of human history, numbers have been a source of information and understanding about people and the world around them. Numerology—the science of divining information about life through numbers—has been around for at least 2,500 years. That's when Pythagoras, a Greek mathematician born in the sixth century B.C.E., created the Pythagorean Number System.

Pythagoras was a mathematician, philosopher, and theorist whose research on numbers gave rise to the science of Numerology. A major influence in Western thought, he is regarded as the founder of the science of geometry, especially the Pythagorean theorem, the formula for a triangle. But most importantly, Pythagoras was the first person to realize that numbers are the very foundation of the universe—something modern physicists simply take for granted.

While Pythagoras is an authentic historical figure, many aspects of his life are shrouded in myth and mystery.

We are certain that Pythagoras was born in the sixth century B.C.E., in Samos, Greece. Most reports agree that he lived a full 100 years. Early in his life his search for truth took him to Egypt, where he studied with the Chaldeans. It is believed he stayed there some twenty-two years, developing his influential mathematical theories.

Pythagoras started his own formal school of philosophy in Croton, Italy, around 525 B.C.E. The first tenet of the Pythagorean Society was that at its deepest level, reality is mathematical in nature. Pythagoras believed that the world was built on the power of numbers; everything that was seen and unseen could be reduced to numbers.

During his time, it was widely accepted that the universe was created from vibrating energy, something the modern scientist might call a wavelength or electromagnetic energy. The characteristics of this energy could be understood through numbers: Each number vibrated in a certain way, and at its core all matter is made up of this vibrating numerological energy. Since Pythagoras taught that each number had a numerical attribute that was unique, all it would take to understand the qualities of a person, place, or thing would be to know which numbers made up its vibrating energy.

Something of this theory has come down to us through the years, not just in Numerology, but in the thought of such disparate thinkers as Plato, who had carved over the door of his academy the words: *Don't enter here if you don't know geometry.* Plato, born in the following century, and widely known as Greece's greatest philosopher, openly acknowledged his debt to Pythagoras.

The astronomer Johannes Kepler (1571–1630) opined that *God is geometry.* Several hundred years later the abstract painter Paul Klee (1879–1940) explained to those who rejected modern art *that it is not the forms we respond to in art, but the geometric shapes beneath the forms.* As I write these words there is a show at the Los Angeles County Museum of the work of Jasper Johns, who for several years painted nothing but numbers. He was entranced by the idea that while the artist can represent everything else, you really cannot represent a number by anything but a number: It is the irreducible element, the building block. Understanding the unseen and underlying patterns—or numbers—of life is the secret to understanding life itself.

Pythagoras believed that the vibration or "tone" of the universe at the exact moment of birth has an influence over both a person's character and his/her destiny in life. This numerological "blueprint" places each human into a classification from Level 1 (characterized primarily by learning about the self) to Level 9 (characterized primarily by learning selflessness). Pythagoras' under-

standing of the numerical vibrations as they apply to humans is only now beginning to be fully appreciated as a science. His greatest aim was to show the
world that numbers have the power to bring all of life into unity and harmony.
It is my privilege to share this science with you, in the hopes that you will be
able to realize this same goal in your own life.

▪ HOW NUMEROLOGY WORKS ▪

Before we go any further, I want to make it clear that Numerology does not depend on psychic ability. It is not clairvoyance. I believe everyone is somewhat
psychic and that we all have intuitions, but the power of Numerology doesn't
depend on these characteristics.

The science of Numerology begins with five primary numbers: two that
can be derived from your birthday, and three that come from your name. These
five numbers, along with a sixth number called the Attitude Number, offer us
insight into who we are and how we can improve our lives.

As I said above, there are five primary numbers and one secondary number
that we'll be working with in this book. These numbers are:

The Soul Number:	Describes what you feel inside. People may not see this part of your character, but you feel it.
The Personality Number:	Describes how people will perceive you. It is what you show the world.
The Power Name Number:	Describes the strength of your name.
The Birth Day Number:	Describes the way others see you.
The Life Path Number:	Describes the path your life must take in order for you to be happy; this is the most important number in your chart!
The Attitude Number (a secondary number, but still very important):	Describes your general attitude toward life.

Note: If your Attitude Number is a Toxic Number to your Life Path Number,
then you will confuse the people in your life. Let people know about this duality right up front.

The most important number in your chart is your Life Path Number. When you don't have a lot of time to figure someone out, this is the number you need to know. Throughout the book when I list the numbers in a particular person's chart, the numbers always come in the same order and **the Life Path Number will always be in bold type.** The chart looks like this:

3369**8**, Attitude 6

The order of the numbers in the chart will always be the same, no matter where you see it in the book. The numbers will always be listed in this order from left to right:

Soul Number
Personality Number
Power Name Number
Birth Day Number
Life Path Number
Attitude Number

You might want to bookmark this page for easy reference, so you'll always know where to find this order if you forget it. But remember: The Life Path Number is the most important number in a chart, and it will **always be in bold.**

▪ POSITIVE AND NEGATIVE ENERGY ▪

One of the first questions people ask me is whether I can tell if they're compatible with their loved ones, coworkers, and significant others, and the answer is yes. Still, when you research the people in your life you may find that you don't get along with someone whose Life Path Number is supposed to be compatible with yours. This is because each number has a positive and a negative energy associated with it. You might be bringing out the negative energy of a particular person's number simply because that's what you're *expecting* from that person—that's what you're used to. This is just one more way that knowing the numbers can help you change your life for the better. Once you know whom you're compatible with, you can start breaking these patterns of low expectations. That's why I want you to break down the numbers of all the people in your life. When you understand the positive and negative side of the numbers, relationships that were a mystery before start making sense. And believe me, as soon as you start using this system, you'll see how accurate it is.

▪ NUMBERS ARE ALL AROUND YOU ▪

Numerology is a whole different way of looking at life. For example, I got a kick out of a recent trip I took. Both my Birth Day Number and my Life Path Number add up to a 3 vibration, which makes me a double 3. On that trip I flew out on flight 33. Interesting, I thought. Then they put me in the 12th row—which, you'll soon learn, breaks down to a 3 as well. When I arrived at my hotel, I was on the 21st floor. Can you guess? Another 3. Then when I flew back, they put me in seat 30—a 3 again—and I wondered what the heck was going on. When the pilot announced that we would be flying at 33,000 feet, I just laughed! It's so fascinating how often the energy speaks to you.

▪ MY STORY ▪

I've done Numerology for nineteen years. The number one question I'm asked by people is, "What made you get into Numerology in the first place?" The answer is—what else?—heartbreak.

He wasn't perfect, but he was my first love. Although I wasn't necessarily happy in the relationship, I was devastated when it was over.

For two years I carried a terrible ache in my heart. I couldn't shake the feeling that I really belonged with him. One day I went to see a Numerologist. She studied my numbers, and those of my lost love. Almost immediately she zeroed in on his family. She asked if I had felt particularly comfortable with them.

> ### NUMBER, VIBRATION, ENERGY
>
> In Numerology, there are three interchangeable words. They are **number**, **vibration**, and **energy**. You will find that I use all three throughout this book when describing the various traits of a person.

I said yes—because one of the things I loved most about my relationship with this man was spending time with his mother and sister. The Numerologist nodded. As a double 3, she said, I was naturally attracted to other 3s. Both his mother and sister had 3s in their charts, and when I felt that energy, it made me feel safe, loved, and fulfilled. She made me understand that the ache in my heart was not for him, but for the comfort of the compatible vibrations.

That day was a turning point for me. After two years of not being able to get over him, my broken heart started to heal. What she'd told me made perfect sense, and I stopped feeling the pain of loss. Instead, I started studying the people in my life through Numerology. My friends, family, and even acquaintances all became case studies for me. It got to the point where I could accurately guess a person's Birth Day Number after only knowing them for a few minutes. Once I got just a few pieces of information, their Number would become obvious to me. I could tell people very specific details about their behavior, their goals, and their strengths.

I even found myself offering career advice based on Numerology, which was ironic since I didn't know where my own career was going at the time. I'd spent most of my adult life searching for my true calling. I'd done television, comedy, and singing—all great careers for a 3 Life Path—but I was never truly fulfilled. My mother once made the comment, "Glynis, no matter how successful you are, you'll never be satisfied." I responded, "That's not true, Mom. I know I have something special to offer, and when it happens for me, I'll know what it is."

About that time, a friend asked me to be a guest on a radio program to talk about Numerology. As soon as I came on the air, the phone lines started ringing and wouldn't stop. I was supposed to do twenty minutes on the air; instead, I was on for three hours.

The show ended at 4 o'clock in the morning, but I didn't leave the station until 5:00 A.M. because everyone—the DJs, the engineers—was asking me to do their numbers. I remember hearing the morning birds singing, and a voice inside me said: "This is it." It was a beautiful feeling.

From that point forward, I have had true peace in my soul. I remembered all the years of aching and wanting something so badly that wasn't happening for me. I had always envisioned telling millions of people: "No matter what you want to achieve, no one can stop you but you." There's a saying, "We are never given a dream without also being given the means to realize it." I am living proof.

I started out in standup comedy because for the short time I was up onstage, I had the power to make people happy. As I began to study Numerology, I found that I not only made people happy for a moment, but for a lifetime. For me, there was no comparison.

Now, while Numerology is not a religion and people of all belief systems can benefit from its power, I want you to know where I'm coming from. I am a spiritual person; I believe in God and pray every day. As human beings we get tired when we believe there's nobody but us we can rely on. That's when the ego takes over. (My favorite definition of EGO is Edging God Out.) My belief in God is a gift that lets me share the power of Numerology without tiring out. After doing over 9,000 readings and counseling others every single day, I'm not exhausted at all. I find it very invigorating because I believe it's a gift from God. He uses me as a vehicle, and gives me the strength I need.

Through Numerology I've helped people look at their numbers, see exactly what their gifts are, and fulfill their dreams. I help my clients change the way they think, so they can manifest their very best selves in life. I am so happy to share this process with you as well. If you keep an open mind, you will find Numerology is easy to understand, simple to put to use, and can transform your life.

Two

Discovering Your Numbers

Numbers are a part of our world, so it's not surprising that numerical references have made their way into everyday language. When I'm happy, I might say I'm "on cloud 9." When I'm out of sorts I feel "at 6s and 7s." An impossible situation is a "Catch-22." There is a good numerological reason for each of these sayings. The 9 is the most evolved number in Numerology, so it's not a surprise that cloud 9 is a good place to be. (Or that a fashionably clad person is "dressed to the 9s.") The 6 and the 7 are Toxic to each other in Numerology, so it is perfectly understandable why we use these particular digits to describe a situation where we feel confused and uncomfortable. The number 22 is one of two "Master Numbers"; feeling out of control, like in a Catch-22 situation, is the surest path to misery for a Master Number 22.

If it seems like I'm leaving out the most obvious example—13—it's because

I have news for those of you who are superstitious: 13 is actually a 4 in numerology, and is not necessarily considered bad luck. It is a number that is there
to remind us to pay attention to all the small details to avoid any possible
mishaps. As you can see, we naturally use numbers to communicate. The more
you study Numerology, the more you'll start to see the power of numbers in our
world.

▪ THE BASICS OF NUMEROLOGY ▪

Each person's numerological chart is a blueprint of who they really are. The
numbers in your chart describe the essence of you—how you behave in certain
situations, what your strengths and weaknesses are, what hurdles you must
overcome to achieve happiness, and how you can improve the quality of your
life. Once you understand the basic principles of how to read your chart, the
power of the numbers is in your hands.

▪ REDUCING TO SINGLE DIGITS ▪

Every number in Numerology has a distinct and special definition. No matter
where you find a particular number in your chart, **the definition of the number
does not change.** By the end of this book it will be possible to have each number's traits committed to memory.

Sound impossible to memorize the meaning behind every single number in
the universe? Well, you don't have to. That's because in Numerology, every
number—from your age, to your date of birth, right up to the longest number
you can think of—can be easily reduced to a *single digit.* So the only numbers
we need to remember are the single digits 1, 2, 3, 4, 5, 6, 7, 8, and 9. (Okay,
there are two other numbers that matter, 11 and 22, but we'll learn about those
later.)

Reducing a number to its single digit is easy—just add the individual digits
that make up the number you are reducing. Here's an example using the number 19:

1) Add up the digits in the number: $1 + 9 = 10$
2) The result here is greater than one digit, so repeat by adding up the two digits in the answer: $1 + 0 = 1$

In Numerology, the number 19 reduces to a 1.

▪ THE PYTHAGOREAN SYSTEM ▪

Once you've learned how to reduce, you now know what it takes to break down the numbers of your full birth date. But in Numerology we also need to know how to break down the numbers in names. To do this, we must travel back 2,500 years and use Pythagoras' system for assigning a number to each letter of the alphabet. The chart is shown below.

PYTHAGOREAN NUMBER SYSTEM

1	2	3	4	5	6	7	8	9
A	B	C	D	E	F	G	H	I
J	K	L	M	N	O	P	Q	R
S	T	U	V	W	X	Y	Z	

EXCEPTION:

If **Y** is next to a consonant (on both sides), it is considered a vowel.

If **Y** is next to a vowel (on either side), it is considered a consonant.

Example:

Joyce: The **Y** is a consonant because it is next to the vowel O.

Gwyneth: The **Y** is a vowel because it is between the two consonants W and N.

▪ THE PRIMARY NUMBERS ▪

As I've said before, in my Numerology readings I focus on the five numbers that describe our most important character traits—I call them the Primary Numbers—plus a sixth "Attitude Number." These numbers are derived from two sources: your name and your date of birth. They are:

1) THE SOUL NUMBER: The numeric value of all the vowels added together in the name that we go by.
2) THE PERSONALITY NUMBER: The numeric value of all the consonants added together in the name that we go by.
3) THE POWER NAME NUMBER: The sum of the Soul Number and the Personality Number added together and reduced to one digit.
4) THE BIRTH DAY NUMBER: The number of the day on which you were born.
5) **THE LIFE PATH NUMBER: The sum of the digits in a person's birth date, including the month, day, and full year.**
6) THE ATTITUDE NUMBER: The sum of the digits in the day and month of your birth date.

Before I get into the specifics of what each of these numbers says about you, let's break down some numbers together. Here's someone we're all familiar with—Tom Cruise. Of course, feel free to work on your own numbers as we go along. You may want to get a notebook and a pencil handy for use throughout the book.

LIFE PATH NUMBER: We will break down the Life Path first because it's the most important number in our lives. The Life Path is the sum of the digits in a person's birth date, including the month, day, and year.

Tom Cruise's birth date is 7/3/1962:

$7 + 3 + 1 + 9 + 6 + 2$

$= 28$

$= 2 + 8$

$= 10$

$= 1 + 0$

$= 1$

Tom Cruise is a 1 Life Path.

BIRTH DAY NUMBER: The Birth Day Number is the day you were born on. Tom Cruise was born on July 3. Since 3 is already a single digit, we don't have to reduce.

Tom Cruise's Birth Day Number is 3.

SOUL NUMBER: The Soul Number is the numeric value of the vowels in the name that we go by. If you look at the Pythagorean chart on page 11 you'll see that the vowels in Tom Cruise's name have the following values:

```
6       39 5
|       ||| |
TOM  CRUISE
```

To get the Soul Number, we add these vowels together and reduce:

$6 + 3 + 9 + 5 = 23$

$2 + 3 = 5$

Tom Cruise has a Soul Number of 5.

PERSONALITY NUMBER: To find our Personality Number we total the numeric value of the consonants in the name that we go by.

TOM CRUISE
| | || |
2   4 39   1

2 + 4 + 3 + 9 + 1 = 19
1 + 9 = 10
1 + 0 = 1
Tom Cruise's Personality Number is a 1.

POWER NAME NUMBER: To get the Power Name Number, you add the Soul Number and the Personality Numbers together. In this case, Tom Cruise's Soul Number is 5, and his Personality Number is 1.

5 + 1 = 6
6 is Tom Cruise's Power Name Number.

ATTITUDE NUMBER: To break down your Attitude Number, simply add together the numerals that make up the month and day of your birth. Again, Tom was born on July 3.

7 + 3 = 10
1 + 0 = 1
Tom Cruise's Attitude Number is 1.

Using the above formulas, Tom's Primary Numbers are 51631, plus an Attitude Number of 1. Here is a quick read on Tom Cruise:

Starting with the 5 in his Soul, Tom likes adventure, beauty, excitement, and that would explain his love of racing.

His Personality Number is a 1, which means he is competitive and likes to win. He's a hard worker but never knows how good he really is.

The 6 is his Power Name Number, the father number, always taking care of other people. This would explain why he has adopted children. And 6s also must manage, or run, their own business or they will not be happy. He has an incredibly successful movie production company.

His Birth Day Number is 3. The 3 is the communicator, the performer. Whether it is acting, singing, counseling, or radio broadcasting, the 3 must be communicating through vocal expression.

His 1 Life Path Number means he has to be independent. He needs a lot of positive feedback. He never stops moving. When 1s finish an assignment, they are on to the next. They do not rest on their laurels. Their mission—should they choose to accept it—is to be number one at everything they do. (That is a little *Mission Impossible* joke in case you missed it. I couldn't resist!) Add to this the fact that Tom also has a 1 Attitude Number and the mystery as to how he has stayed on top all of these years in Hollywood is solved. Judging by Tom's chart, he will continue to be number 1 at whatever he sets his sights on.

> ## WHICH NAME SHOULD I USE?
>
> What do you do if the name you use on a daily basis is not the same name that's on your birth certificate? For example, your birth certificate might say Jonathan Stanley Morris, but you go by the name Jon Morris. *The first name you should break down is the one you go by on a daily basis.* If you're a married woman and you took your husband's name, use it—whatever you go by most often. Note that we'll talk more about your birth certificate name when we discuss Destiny numbers in chapter 7.

▪ CHARACTERISTICS OF EACH NUMBER ▪

All right, that's enough about Tom Cruise—now it's time to look at *you*! By now I hope you've done a breakdown of each number and have come up with your five Primary Numbers, plus your Attitude Number. The next few chapters will take a look at each of these six important numbers, explaining how they relate to your life. Before we get there, however, I want to remind you that no matter where a number falls in your chart, its general traits are the same. The qualities of a 3 are consistent, whether we're talking about your Soul Number, your Attitude Number, or even your home address. Below is a brief description for each of the nine numbers, based on very broad characteristics. Within the

chapters that follow you'll find longer descriptions tailored to their particular role in your life—i.e., what it means to have a Life Path of 8, a Power Name of 5, etc.

GENERAL CHARACTERISTICS FOR EACH NUMBER VIBRATION

A 1 Vibration denotes independence, self-motivation, and a need to be in charge.

A 2 Vibration is sensitive and doesn't like conflict.

A 3 Vibration values communication and creative energy.

A 4 Vibration is solid, responsible, and seeks security.

A 5 Vibration seeks freedom and adventure.

A 6 Vibration is a nurturing vibration that tends to be a caretaker.

A 7 Vibration seeks the truth and is always asking the big question, "Who am I?"

An 8 Vibration needs financial and spiritual freedom.

A 9 Vibration exudes leadership and humanitarian instincts.

Three

The Life Path Number

You can have anything you want, if you want it desperately enough. You must want it with an inner exuberance that erupts through the skin and joins the energy that created the world.

—SHEILAH GRAHAM

The most significant vibration is your Life Path Number, and that is what you should study first. Simply put, the Life Path Number is the number you must act upon in order to be truly happy.

By "act upon," I mean that this number's qualities must be allowed to play themselves out in your life. For example, 5 Life Paths are Adventurers, and seek freedom. If they get married at a very young age and feel tied down, chances are the marriage will not be a lasting one. An 8 Life Path—the Executive—will not feel happy and fulfilled until they have established some financial security.

Since the Life Path Number paves the way for the rest of our lives to unfold, it deserves a lot of attention. While I'll give brief descriptions for each of the other five Primary Numbers in the chapters that follow, the Life Path Number gives more information about a person than any of the others.

▪ NUMBER GROUPS ▪

Each of the nine Life Path Numbers can be categorized as a mind number, a creative number, or a business number. These categories are called Natural Match Numbers.

> 1-5-7 *are Mind Numbers, always thinking.*
> 3-6-9 *are Creative Numbers, always creating.*
> 2-4-8 *are Business Numbers, always taking care of business.*

▪ THE MIND NUMBERS: 1-5-7 ▪

The 1-5-7s are always thinking. They are often well educated, enjoy traveling, and need to use their high energy in a healthy way, or that same energy can be destructive. Being surrounded by nature and doing physical exercise are two great ways for these numbers to get out of their heads and enjoy life more. It is easy for the 1-5-7 numbers to fall into the habit of dissecting their partners as though they were science projects. If they marry one of these Natural Match Numbers, they will have a partner of like mind, who will understand—and it won't be a problem.

▪ THE CREATIVE NUMBERS: 3-6-9 ▪

As for the 3-6-9, I think that any blend, 3 with 6 or 6 with 9, are great numbers to be together because they have a creative edge to their character and it can be great fun. There's an understanding without even trying. Whenever a 3 asks, "Who should I be with?" I can always say a 6 or a 9, because I know that, creatively, they click. The 3-6-9 appreciates and often performs in the arts, whether it is in painting, dance, theater, etc.

▪ THE BUSINESS NUMBERS: 2-4-8 ▪

In my experience, this means the 2 is in the business of love; the 4 is in the business of security, building their foundation; and the 8 is in the business of

establishing financial freedom and doing things on a grand scale. When the
2 lives on the positive side of its vibration, it has more understanding and
empathy than any other number. They
do want to be friends with everyone.

> Throughout this book you will hear
> me refer to Toxic Numbers and Chal-
> lenge Numbers. They are inter-
> changeable.

My other observation of a 2 is that they are the ones who always recommend
someone who can help you. For instance, if your back hurts, they'll say, "Oh, I
know a chiropractor who would be good for you." Or if you're out of a job: "I
know someone who's looking for someone to help them with their business."
The 2s are constantly trying to refer someone to someone else. Notice how
that's not competitive? They're just trying to help, to make the world a better
place.

Of all the numbers 1 through 9, the two numbers that can really have some
difficult lessons are the Business Numbers 4 and 8. They both learn the hard
way, they have to hit their heads before they learn, and they don't take advice
well so they tend to go through a tough experience. The good news is that when
they overcome it, their rewards are great.

▪ LIFE PATH DESCRIPTIONS ▪

As you already know, the Life Path Number gives you more information about
your life than any other number in your chart. This chapter gives you a full ex-
planation of every Life Path Number and its characteristics. At the end of each
Life Path description, I list the numbers of all the other Life Paths and whether
they are a Natural Match, Compatible, a Challenge, or Neutral to you (note
that not every number has a Neutral Number). The numbers in this chapter refer to general compatibility, from family members to coworkers to significant
others. I give you a more in-depth description of your romantic compatibility
with each of the Life Path Numbers in chapter 12.

Remember, to find your Life Path Number you *add the month, day, and
full year of your birth date and break it down to one digit.* Let's use Jack
Nicholson this time as an example.

Jack Nicholson was born 4/22/1937

4 + 2+ 2+ 1+ 9 + 3 + 7 = 28

Notice that you add these numbers straight across, including the 19 from the year. The Life Path is only one digit, so you must continue to break it down.

2 + 8 = 10   1 + 0 = 1

Jack Nicholson is a 1 Life Path.

Do you now know your Life Path Number? Then start learning about yourself in the following Life Path section. *Note that the words Life Path, Energy, and Vibration are synonymous in the following definitions.*

The "1" Life Path:
The Leader

The whole world steps aside for the man who knows where he is going. Winners expect to win in advance. Life is a self-filling prophecy.

—ANONYMOUS

The 1 Life Path is someone who is self-motivated, independent, a hard worker. They have a fierce competitive desire to be the best, and almost always succeed. Unfortunately, they never believe they're as good as they really are, because of what I call their "inner bully." This is the nonstop voice of criticism in their head, telling them they're not good enough. Despite all of their achievements, this voice demands: "What's *wrong* with you? What are you *doing* with your life?" They are extremely critical of themselves, and expect others to live up to their incredibly high standards. If they are disappointed, they are quick to judge.

The Life Path 1 can get involved with all kinds of people and business schemes—even those that prove disastrous—and walk away unscathed, knowing exactly who they are. Jack Nicholson comes to mind because as often as we hear that "Bad Boy Jack" has done something wrong, everyone continues to love and forgive him. The 1's need for individuality is enormous. They are pioneers, innovators, unique, and capable of great success. The 1 Life Paths are an asset to other numbers because these are the people who will push you to strive for excellence as well. You are very likely to want to achieve your own goals because it is so inspiring to watch their ceaseless quest for perfection.

It is difficult for 1s to ask for help because they want to handle the problem their own way. When the 1 Life Path makes up their mind on how they are going to take care of a situation, it's nearly impossible to talk them out of it. This means that occasionally the 1 will fall on their face. If you are a 1, try to listen to others from time to time.

Others may see the 1 Life Path as egotistical or domineering but that's not really where the 1 is coming from. The 1 is just clear on who they are and strong when it comes to offering an opinion. If a 1 feels they are doing well, you will know it by the look of joy on their face. Those with a 1 Life Path can be kind and generous, but if they feel that their partners are being unfaithful or have deceived them in love or business, they can be ruthless.

The 1 vibration needs to be managing in some way—if not running the entire company! They make great entrepreneurs and inventors because of their self-motivation. They are also known for having healing hands, so massage therapy, reflexology, and acupuncture are fields in which they excel. Other fulfilling occupations include: writer, restaurant owner, store owner, trial lawyer, military officer, farmer, or anything that calls for independent action and decision-making. When choosing a career, the 1 Life Path must ask the question: "What is it I've *always wanted to be*?" Once they answer that question and go after their dreams, they are unstoppable. They have tremendous focus, and they always become the very best at whatever they do. The world is their oyster.

At the same time, the 1 vibration is always shooting to be number one, and if they do a great job overall but just one thing goes wrong, they will beat themselves up over it. They always feel like time is moving way too fast. The 1s need to ease up and encourage themselves instead of being too self-critical.

Note that if you're the boss to a 1 Life Path, the worst thing you can do is to stand over their shoulder, watching them work. They have a rebellious streak, and will react badly if they feel you don't have faith in them. Instead, you must let them know you trust them to do an amazing job—and then leave them alone. If you handle them in this way, they'll give you magic.

Another great activity for the 1 is to watch sports, races, game shows— anything where people are *winning*. Dancing is a great release for the 1 Life Path. It helps them get out of their heads and relax. Yoga is a popular meditation technique and will also have a soothing effect.

NATURAL MATCH NUMBERS: *1, 5, and 7*
COMPATIBLE NUMBERS: *2, 3, and 9*
CHALLENGE NUMBERS: *4, 6, and 8*

David Letterman is the perfect example of the 1 Life Path. Letterman has been a talk show host for the past twenty-one years, and although his ratings slipped to second place (when Hugh Grant made the infamous appearance on Jay Leno), his show always wins the Emmy in the Best Talk Show category. Even in sickness Dave is number one: When he had to get quintuple heart bypass surgery, the entire country was on alert, following every report about his health. His fiercely loyal following stuck with him even in his absence. He came back to more viewers than ever and much less ratings pressure from the honchos at CBS. David's life work, courage, and quest for excellence have made him number one in America's heart. What more could a 1 Life Path ask for?

The "2" Life Path: The Mediator

Keep away from people who try to belittle your ambitions. Small people always do that, but the really great make you feel that you, too, can become great.

—MARK TWAIN

This 2 Life Path is someone who is seeking harmony in life. They are here to love others and to be loved in return. Music has an especially soothing effect on them; they are easygoing; if you want someone who is affectionate, you should seek a 2 Life Path Number because they do like hugs and kisses. They need and give lots of love and affection. Unless all the other numbers in their chart discourage giving such absolute love, it is their natural way.

The 2s are mediators, they loathe conflict, and they will do whatever it takes to avoid it. If there are people in their lives who are fighting, they'll try to fix it. 2s also tend to be psychic, and they will have dreams that come true. They also experience déjà vu. It's never a problem for them to follow, a 2 doesn't have to be the leader. Because of their natural psychic ability, they tend to be good at Astrology, Numerology, Tarot reading, Tea leaf reading, and the I Ching. They make good counselors and social workers. These people have concern for others, enjoy their company, and don't like to be alone. They crave unconditional love, and make great parents, the kind who tend to be friends to their children.

The 2 does not need the spotlight. They'll do the job. As a matter of fact, they are the people who would donate to a charity in secret. They would just do it out of the kindness of their heart. They need to bring people together and they're the ones to see when looking for anything from a dentist to a carpenter. They know everyone and love to help out. The only time 2s get angry is if they feel pushed or threatened. Otherwise, they're extremely good-natured.

If you look into a 2's eyes, you can just see what good, kind people they are. That is just where they come from. The flip side of a 2 is that now and then you might meet a 2 who feels they do everything for everybody and they feel drained. Yet, if you know them personally, you may feel they are giving themselves far too much credit.

I think it's important, when it comes to a 2, to keep in mind that they are here to love others and to be loved in return. If you work with them, they will definitely come through for you. The 2 has to be careful not to take on the problems of the people they love. My analogy for the 2 is that if they saw someone fall in a well and cry for help, the 2 would jump in and ask, "What's wrong?" only to look up and say, "Oh my goodness, now we're both in here!"

So it is important for the 2 to have empathy, but to, nevertheless, be able to stand back and say: "Okay, I'm sorry that happened, but it's still your problem. I'll help as much as I can, but I am not going to get in it with you." The 2 has to be careful not to place themselves completely at another's disposal, because eventually they will get angry and resentful. They often worry about what others think of them; here's a reminder for all of us, but especially the 2: "What people think of me is none of my business."

When the 2 is surrounded by emotional vampires who are taking all of their energy—it's okay for them to just walk away. Otherwise, what they don't deal with mentally will eventually attack them physically, and that's why a 2 Life Path can wind up with health problems. Easygoing as they usually are, when they get upset, it is like a volcano erupting. When this emotional outburst is over, they will feel very drained, because anger is so toxic to the very essence of who they are. Because of this, 2s must be careful with whom they spend their time.

NATURAL MATCH NUMBERS: *2, 4, and 8*
COMPATIBLE NUMBERS: *1, 3, 6, and 9*
CHALLENGE NUMBERS: *5 and 7*

Meg Ryan is a solid example of the 2 Life Path. Her loving 2 nature comes through on screen and has earned her a place in the pantheon of America's foremost sweethearts. Meg is best known for her heartbreaking romantic comedies, and her best work has been in movies about love—just think of *Sleepless in Seattle* and *When Harry Met Sally*. The classic 2 has an open face that shows every emotion, with kind eyes and a contagious laugh—practically a portrait of Meg Ryan. She exudes a wonderful loving quality whenever she's on screen. Her personal life follows the number 2 profile as well. When her marriage ended, I knew as a Numerologist that she and Dennis Quaid had numbers that were extremely challenging to each other, and that the marriage was incredibly hard on both of them. When the media attacked her for her brief love affair with costar Russell Crowe, it left her emotionally depleted. Since her divorce from Dennis, she has been trying to be open to new love, which isn't easy for the 2. When 2s get their hearts broken, it's hard for them to get back out there and really trust again. But they must—because without love, a 2 can never be truly content.

The "3" Life Path:
The Communicator

The best way to succeed in life is to act on the advice we give to others.

—ANONYMOUS

When Shakespeare wrote that "all the world's a stage," he was talking like a 3. When on track, the 3 Life Path is always performing or taking center stage in some way. The 3s love creativity, communication, and connecting with people. They are often the entertainers of the world. They love being listened to, so you'll often find them on the phone. Writing is also a big deal to the 3, as it's another form of communication. Anything having to do with the written word is appealing to this vibration.

In personal relationships, 3s can also be very romantic. They are fiercely loyal, and they never truly get over their past relationships. Even when the relationship ends, for a 3 it's never quite over.

When the 3 Life Paths aren't expressing themselves creatively, they will manifest some sort of drama. They sometimes embellish what's going on to make their lives seem more interesting. Watch a child who's a 3 at their storytelling and you'll notice they always exaggerate. The same can be said for 3 vibration adults! If they use this tendency in a positive way, channeling it into motivational speaking, singing, or acting, they can keep it healthy.

The 3 Life Path needs people. When they go home to check their messages and there are none, they can feel a real sense of rejection. In relationships, 3 Life Paths don't always see the situation for what it really is until they get burned. Since 3s are natural counselors who see the potential in others, they often pick a partner who is a "patient," with the thought that they can save that person. This tendency often leads them into depression. Everything is going great one minute and the next, BOOM! The 3 crash-lands. The 3 Life Paths have to guard against extreme highs and lows. They must learn to control their emotions, and look for the middle ground.

A 3 Life Path makes an excellent salesperson. If a 3 believes in something, by the time he or she is through with you, you will believe in it too. The 3s make great entertainers, models, actors, designers, musicians, singers, comedians, and any type of performer. They also shine in the worlds of cosmetology, hairdressing, fashion, and jewelry design. The reason is simple: They want the world to look better. They take a look at someone and say, "How can I make that person better-looking and special?" These people are natural clowns. People who come to my mind are Bill Cosby, Groucho Marx, and Tracey Ullman. These are the people who want to enjoy life, and never quite grow up.

The creative 3 vibration doesn't do well with the standard nine-to-five job, and doesn't like working under others. Their minds move very quickly and when someone is slow thinking, it will frustrate the 3. At the same time, the 3 must guard against becoming too domineering when they are in charge. If they are in a dead-end job or lifestyle, they can get themselves caught in some pretty sticky situations that may be hard to get out of. They have to use their creative gifts. They can seem manic-depressive, experiencing intense mood swings if they're not using their talents.

A 3 Life Path must be careful with whom they spend their time. They are warm and giving by nature and tend to attract world-class takers. If 3s find that they are always the giver in a relationship and there is no reciprocation, it will lead to bitterness. They *must* learn to walk away from relationships that are unbalanced in this way.

Their strength of mind and sharp wit often put them ahead of the crowd. When the 3 Life Path is living on the positive side of its vibration, the 3 is clever, entertaining, and makes for great company. They are a joy to be around. The 3s are known for their trademark smile, bright eyes, and pleasant-sounding voice. If they are living on the negative side of the vibration, they can spread gossip and have a very difficult time keeping a secret. If you are a 3, learning to bite your tongue would be wise. One of the gifts a 3 does possess is to take an adverse condition and flip it around to the benefit of themselves and others. The 3s learn from adversity, intuitively understanding that sometimes you have to go through the negative to get to the positive. The 3 Life Path uses that fine sense of humor to get through the bad days. Laughter is what saves them.

If you are a 3 Life Path and you are reading this thinking, Wow, I'm not like that, I don't feel like I can express myself at all, this automatically tells me that you have scars from your original family; that your parents, no matter how caring, did not give you that round of applause that you so needed as a child. I strongly recommend that you go to chapter 4 and do the affirmations for the number 3. It is important for you to heal yourself so that you can be the person you were born to be. Trust that you can find your way to effortless self-expression, and you will. It's never too late!

NATURAL MATCH NUMBERS: *3, 6, and 9*
COMPATIBLE NUMBERS: *1, 2, and 5*
CHALLENGE NUMBERS: *4, 7, and 8*

Barbara Walters is an ideal example of the 3 Life Path. The 3 is the communicator, who is here on the earth to motivate and uplift other people. Barbara Walters is famous for asking just the right questions, bringing out the emotional, vulnerable sides of her guests. Under her guidance, the most powerful and famous personalities of our time find themselves opening up in ways they rarely do in public. This ability to engage with others is the gift of the 3 Life Path—more than just a talker, the 3 is the natural counselor, the one who can put you most at ease. Despite being in her seventies, Barbara's career keeps getting better and better. She works a full day, appearing on her hit talk show *The View* in the morning and on *20/20* weekly. Her Oscar specials are "must see" television for most people. This would be a daunting work schedule for anyone, but it's not really work for Barbara. As a 3 Life Path, she loves her career, and would not feel complete without the ability to communicate, share, and be heard in the world.

The "4" Life Path:
The Teacher

Don't wait for your ship to come in, swim out to it.

—ANONYMOUS

The 4 Life Path is a very cerebral, intelligent number. The 4s are seekers of knowledge and born teachers. They often wear glasses, and I think of them as "human computers"—the fact that Bill Gates is a 4 Life Path is no surprise. They are into the logic in life—A plus B *must* equal C.

We learn from 4s. If I said it's a beautiful day with a blue sky, a 4 might add, "Yeah, but do you see that black cloud?" The 4 is not trying to ruin my day; they just want me to see the situation from all sides. I call this the "Spock mentality." They are always seeking truth. While they sometimes come off as cynical, what they are really trying to do is give you information that they think will help you. You've got to take them with good humor, because they really don't mean you any harm. They are actually trying to make your life easier.

The 4 is the first to say, "I don't want to argue"—and yet they always wind up in arguments! Why? I believe it's because they are so honest and they are very direct. They don't often cushion the blow.

The 4 can intuitively fix things and often don't quite know how they do it. Children with this vibration can solve puzzles that would stymie most adults. I knew a 4 Life Path eight-year-old girl who figured out how to adjust the broken door on the family dryer with a safety pin, so it would run until the repairman got there. Young 4s seem wise beyond their years.

The 4 needs lots of positive affirmation and is afraid of criticism. This can mean that when they have a great idea, it often lives and dies in their head because they're reluctant to act on it. They overprocess, saying to themselves, "If I can't do it perfectly, I don't want to do it at all." A lot of their dreams are never achieved as a result. The 4 vibration needs to remember to follow the old Nike slogan: "Just do it."

The home is very important to the 4. They crave the security it brings, and always make an effort to pay their bills on time to protect their haven, the place where they can relax and feel they are safe. This need for stability can backfire, though. The 4 might stay in a bad relationship, because they dislike change of any kind and don't want to leave what feels like security.

All of us would do well to keep a to-do list, but it is absolutely essential for a 4. Their minds are filled with so many different thoughts that unless they keep a list, it's easy to let a couple of things slide by. Once the thoughts are put on paper, the 4s can set their minds at ease and avoid having too much going on in their very busy brains.

Nature's beauty has a calming effect on the 4. They often like to hike and camp; they tend to be very good at gardening and enjoy working in the back-yard. Growing their own food, or making a beautiful garden with flowers they can be proud of, is a very healthy outlet, for the 4 likes to move slowly and de-liberately. They don't want to have anyone pushing them into a situation they don't feel ready for. This Vibration likes to have a plan and they want their lives to be orderly.

If you are involved with a male 4, please note that he definitely wants to be a provider. He needs security for himself, so it makes sense for him to take care of others when he can. If he cannot, depression is sure to follow. You may find that you have no idea what your 4 vibration sweetheart is thinking, because he is so often inside his own head.

The 4 Life Path woman is strong. She's sometimes taken to be a bit "mas-culine" in the sense that she takes care of everything. She is very responsible, and may be the family breadwinner. She will wear makeup and dress beauti-fully, but she has no problem getting down and dirty when she needs to.

A word of caution for the 4: With a mind that's always running at full speed, the temptation arises to drown your thoughts in alcohol. You have so much going on up there and just want to relax.

The 4 vibration must find healthy, positive outlets to help free yourselves from your own overactive minds. Something I often suggest to my clients, espe-cially the 4, is keeping a journal. You can write your thoughts out and purge whatever is troubling you, rather than trying to drown it with an addiction.

There's a very grounded quality to the 4. The average 4 is not obsessed with being filthy rich; they just want to make sure they have enough for the future to feel secure. Because of their desire to protect, you will find 4s in fire-fighting and police work. They are often in some form of construction. They can be architects, builders, or landscapers—any job that has to do with products of the earth. The 4 likes things that are tangible and solid. Building something that can shelter and bring comfort to others appeals to them. Investing in real estate is a good choice for this vibration.

Honesty is crucial to the 4, especially in relationships. When 4s love, they are very sincere about it. If they discover they've been betrayed, they can lose their trust, making it very hard for them to love again. The other type of 4 will concentrate so much on their work and plans for the future, they won't notice the relationship falling apart and will be shocked and devastated when it ends.

In general, the 4 absorbs everything about their surroundings. They see everything, and because of the way they process information, they need their peace and quiet. They have this sensible, traditional, well-behaved way about them. They don't like people who are overly flashy or gregarious. If someone is too loud or obnoxious, they will get offended. The 4 is very selective in their friendships and they don't need a lot of people in their lives. There is a loner quality to the 4, similar to that of the 7.

It is not uncommon for a 4 to have panic attacks. They want the situation they're in to be in absolutely perfect order. Scientists, however, tell us that the natural state of the universe is chaos! They need to embrace this fact and rest assured that things will sort themselves out in the end. Remembering this can make a 4 feel better immediately.

A final thought on the 4 Life Path. The 4 does not like to look naive in any situation. When they learn a skill, they are inclined to become expert at it—that's why 4s make such amazing teachers. So if there's a 4 out there working for someone else and thinking, Boy, I do this better than my boss, then I suggest you start teaching it to other people. You'll make your own money, and finally find true fulfillment.

NATURAL MATCH NUMBERS: *2, 4, and 8*
COMPATIBLE NUMBERS: *6 and 7*
CHALLENGE NUMBERS: *1, 3, 5, and 9*

Oprah Winfrey is by far my favorite example of the 4 Life Path. The 4 is the teacher number. A 4 has an unquenchable thirst for knowledge and an equally strong need to help those around them learn. When Oprah asks a question, you can tell she's just as curious as her audience to know the answer. It can be argued that no one has done more to educate America than Oprah. With Oprah's Book Club, *O, the Oprah Magazine,* and her help in launching the career of Dr. Phil, she has made a tremendous difference in the intellectual and moral climate of her time. Her talk show is truly a classroom; as viewers, we're all students turning on the television to watch the teacher. And just like any smart 4 Life Path, she's managed to amass a vast fortune, ensuring her financial stability along the way.

The "5" Life Path:
The Adventurer

Obstacles are those frightful things you see when you take your eyes
off your goals.

—ANONYMOUS

The 5 Life Path loves freedom, fun, and adventure. They love variety; they
might take a different route to work each day because they get bored so easily.
This vibration needs constant stimulation. They like passion. Escape is the
name of the 5's game; of all the Life Paths, 5s are the most likely to escape
through sex, food, drugs, alcohol, travel, or overwork.

The average 5 Life Path male does not get married early, and if they do, they
often get married more than once. The first marriage is often short-lived because
they don't want to feel tied down. They need to feel it's their world, and if a
woman holds on too tightly or is too needy, they feel smothered. This is also true
for the 5 Life Path woman. She cannot stand a man who clings to her. The
woman's message is very simple: "Do not control me." If you give your 5 sweetheart plenty of space he or she will almost always come back to you.

This Life Path is all about the senses. Things must taste just right, smell
good, look pretty, and feel pleasing, or they're not happy. This goes for their
appearance as well: The 5 likes to look attractive. In Numerology, 3s and 5s are
similar in that they both like to look "performance ready"—hair, clothes, and
makeup just perfect.

The 5s are also our natural detectives. They love to find out what happened,
to be in the know. If they think someone is being dishonest, they'll do the research to find out the truth. They don't like feeling that they're in the dark.

These people are the celebrators of life. The typical 5 loves Thanksgiving,
Christmas, Hanukkah, or any holiday they can find on the calendar. They like
to make every occasion beautiful and exciting. They're also natural givers, and
would rather give the perfect gift than receive it. I often say that if a 5 received
a thank-you note, the 5 would write a thank you for the thank you! The 5s are

also known for their great penmanship and are experts at leaving messages on your answering machine that make you want to call them back. They give just enough information to pique your curiosity.

When it comes to career, 5s make good photojournalists, pilots, flight attendants, travel agents, tour guides, cruise directors—anything to do with travel. I doubt there's a 5 on this planet who wouldn't enter a drawing for a free plane ticket. They're always making plans to go to Europe or somewhere tropical and exciting.

It is important that the 5s venture out and live their quest, be it taking a career they love or traveling all over the world. If they aren't making use of their energy and drive, life can easily turn into a soap opera. This false drama can lead to depression and a martyr complex. If you know a 5 Life Path who feels their life is not their own, you already know that they can become champion complainers.

The adventuresome 5 is often entrepreneurial and doesn't like to be subject to someone else's authority. Since 5s have a natural gift for entertaining, you'll often find them in the hospitality industry. A good profession for the 5 is wedding planning and decorating.

At the same time, there's a wild side to the 5, because they would rather be dead than bored. It's no surprise that you'll often find 5s in the charts of rock stars, strippers, and casino owners. I've yet to meet a 5 whose life was not fascinating and who didn't have more than enough stories for just one lifetime. The 5s are also gamblers. If not risking actual money at the table, they are taking chances in life.

They are compassionate. Any 5 who sees a homeless man wants to know his story. When they see an injustice, they can't help but be affected by it even if it has nothing to do with them personally.

A lot of 5s escape in books. When they read books, they live vicariously through them. Of course, that can be a safe and healthy form of escape. I have also found that 5s make wonderful fiction writers because their imagination is so vivid. When you pick up a book written by a 5 Life Path, you will fall into this imaginary world that they have created, and when the story is over, you will be very eager for their next novel. J. K. Rowling, the author of the Harry Potter novel series, is a 5 Life Path—need I say more? As you can see, escape is the name of their game. If you yell at a 5, the 5 will not listen. A 5 will tune you out. They might shake their head and nod agreeably, but truthfully, they have mentally left the building.

The 5 is restless and has to keep moving. They are quick to jump in and out of relationships, and can be lured away from their partners by the promise of more passion and sex elsewhere. I caution my clients to beware of letting go of a healthy relationship too soon; often 5s will leave a marriage and years later realize it was the best relationship they'd ever had.

People with this Life Path have to live their lives and have fun and experience the variety life has to offer. If you're involved with a 5, my advice is to avoid the temptation to cling too tightly. If your 5 is in a job that requires that he or she has to leave you from time to time, just let go. You don't need to feel threatened; just trust that you are loved. And when your 5 comes back, you'll have more love and appreciation than ever before.

NATURAL MATCH NUMBERS: *1, 5, and 7*
COMPATIBLE NUMBERS: *3 and 9*
CHALLENGE NUMBERS: *2, 4, and 6*
NEUTRAL NUMBERS: *8*

Fashion designer Bob Mackie is a very good example of the 5 Life Path. Mackie has dressed some of the world's most fabulous women for events like the Oscars and the Golden Globes—a perfect career for the 5, who wants the world, and all the people in it, to be *gorgeous*. The 5 encourages those around them to make that extra-special effort to bring beauty into the world—whether it's through their hair, their makeup, or their homes. When you're wearing a Bob Mackie gown, you're ready to party—which is also fitting for the 5 Life Path, who is the celebrator in this life. It's no surprise that Mackie has recently branched out into fragrances and furniture design, since the 5 is always on the go, trying new things. But no matter what kind of creation he's working on, the goal is the same: making the world a beautiful place to live in. He is using all of his creative talents and staying busy—just the way the 5 Life Path would want it to be.

The "6" Life Path:
The Nurturer

When I was a child, my mother said to me, "If you become a soldier, you'll be a general. If you become a monk, you'll end up as the pope." Instead, I became a painter and wound up as Picasso.

—PABLO PICASSO

The 6 Life Path is the natural parent, viewing others from a paternal or maternal point of view. A 6 Life Path goes along with love and marriage like the proverbial "horse and carriage."

There is a nurturing quality to the 6. If the 6 can't have children, chances are they'll teach schoolchildren—or run a big business and treat their *employees* like children! If a 6 Life Path woman divorces, she often throws herself into the lives of her children and has difficulty ever seeing them as grownups. In her mind, her son or daughter will be a child forever. Of course, now and again I'll meet a 6 man who says he has no desire for children. When I hear this, I automatically ask him if he has any pets. That's when he'll light up like a proud parent, and tell me all about his cat, dog, horse, etc. So I suggest to you 6s out there who aren't going to be the parent of a child to find a pet to love, hold, and hug. You won't believe the difference it will make in your life.

In terms of romantic relationships, it comes as no surprise that 6 women, especially those who don't have children of their own, tend to attract men who act like little boys. The 6 man, on the other hand, attracts women who are damsels in distress. But even above marriage, domestic tranquility is paramount to the 6. If they are with a partner who displays anger or generally causes a lot of unpleasantness—especially around the children—they usually decide they'd rather be alone than keep that partner around.

A 6 Life Path must find ways to use their creative energies. Art, music, and poetry are natural avenues to take. If 6s don't keep busy, they can get caught up in petty things—such as gossiping and redecorating the home over and over again—just because they're bored. Because 6s so believe in a strong family unit, if happily married, they would rather spend time with their partners than with friends.

If the 6 has not made the choice to have a family, then the workplace is the home, and his employees and coworkers become the family. The 6 Life Path will provide the same kind of nurturing presence at the office or in a home environment.

These are magnetic people. They tend to be physically attractive, but it's more than that—there's a force about them that's hard to ignore. The 6 needs to manage or own their own company. They find it hard to work for other people.

Thoughts and words are powerful for all Life Paths, but they can be especially problematic for the 6. As someone who is predisposed to be a parent, a 6 is concerned with making sure the future is going to be taken care of. Often, this means a 6 woman will assure herself that, if necessary, she would be able to make it on her own. When a married woman starts to say this to herself, the next thing you know she's divorced. And yes, she can take care of business and make it, but she's suddenly alone when she didn't need to be. Thoughts are very powerful and will attract whatever we believe we are going to get, so I tell 6s not to say this kind of thing. As Job lamented in the Bible: "The thing I greatly feared has come upon me."

This is something I see over and over. One 6 client told me that every man she had been involved with had cheated on her. Well, just in knowing she thought about this regularly, I knew she was attracting men who would cheat on her. It wasn't something she was choosing consciously, but it was a direct result of having this limited belief.

The 6 needs harmony. Unfortunately, they often forget that they must deal with their own unhappiness before they try to fix life for others. When the 6 is in trouble, they just need to speak up and say what they're feeling when they're feeling it.

The 6's home is everything. They are the natural interior decorators, and like to rearrange their homes and make them just right. If they are ever in a position where they have to live in somebody else's house, they are unfulfilled.

In my observations of 6 vibration women, time and again their keen sense of smell comes up in conversation. Oftentimes they can't wear perfume because it's overwhelming to them. They tend to be particular about the scents and lotions they use and those used by the people around them. If someone is smoking in a building, the 6 can smell it across the hall. One client who took a daily fitness walk on a certain street noticed an unbearable odor. It got to the point where she had to change her route to avoid the general area. Two months later the police discovered a dead body in the trunk of a car on that block—the 6 had been able to smell the decomposing body just two days after the murder.

When you have a 6-vibration child, you may find that they act as if *he or she* is the parent, in charge of *you*. Don't take it personally; just work with these children and provide ways for them to use their nurturing qualities, such as getting a pet to take care of. Life Path 6 children may not get the memo on the fact that you are older and wiser, but they are dynamic and destined to do something great if you are supportive of them.

A perfect day for a 6 would be if the people in their life got on their knees and said, "I'm not worthy." Okay, maybe not quite that dramatic, but it's true that 6s don't take criticism well. If you have a 6 in your life, you must find a way to compliment them prior to offering constructive criticism. If the 6 is a child, you might say something like, "Gee, your room looks really good. You've kept it clean and I'm really proud of you." Only then can you go on to the objective. If math is the problem, say: "Could you please work on your math a little bit harder?" Because if you have praised the child first, he'll be more open to listening—and hearing—what you have to say. (Actually, I would recommend this technique for all numbers.) There are some numbers that verbally come right out with the negative that they are feeling and it hurts people. I know that's rarely deliberate. I really think most of us are trying to help each other, and defensiveness is what gets in the way of true communication. If you put that compliment first, it is the way to communicate because then others can really hear you.

When it comes to friendship, 6s tend to be loyal and trustworthy; if you confide in them they will keep your secrets. The only time the 6 will betray your trust is if they are living on the negative side of the number. The upside is that if a 6 does betray your trust, and is confronted, they will feel worse than you do. The 6 will continue to ask for forgiveness until you decide to let him or her back into your life. If you choose not to forgive, the 6 will always carry the pain of having let you down. Betrayal is that contrary to the essence of the 6 Life Path.

So to the 6 Life Path I would say to be careful not to give away confidential information, as the act will have a boomerang effect on you. After all, as a 6 Life Path you very much need to have people respect your privacy—confidentiality means a great deal to you. Remember The Golden Rule and do unto others as you would have them do unto you.

Occupations that work for the 6 include interior decorator, real estate agent, guidance counselor, academic adviser, and greeting card designer. They also excel as hair and makeup artists. Many 6s are creatively gifted, and if that's true for you, you should rejoice and be sure to work with it. We find many 6s acting and making music, whether by playing an instrument or singing.

There is only so much room a person can give in a relationship—and the 6 Life Path often tries to push that limit by giving too much. The result is that the 6 puts people on a pedestal. Unfortunately, anyone who's up on a pedestal is bound to fall at one time or another. Next thing you know, 6s feel betrayed and will often begin to see themselves as martyrs. One of the great talents of the 6 is the ability to make others feel very guilty.

Once the 6 believes they are carrying most of the burden in a relationship, they'll break it off abruptly—and leave their partner wondering what went wrong. For this reason 6s can't wait too long before they speak up. I would caution the 6 to keep communication open before things go terribly wrong. The sudden anger you can display will come as a huge surprise to the recipient, and often can mean the downfall of the relationship. When a 6 is unhappy, no one in the room is happy. Everyone around the table feels a little bit sick as they eat the turkey that the unhappy 6 just cooked.

What is interesting about a 6 is that people usually sense a compassionate personality, but if the 6 decides they do not like you, or if they're not comfortable in a setting, they can put up an air that is so cold, it will chill the most thick-skinned person. This is the kind of power a 6 has. And the 6 *always* has an opinion.

A 6 Life Path believes that "if you want something done, you have to do it yourself." They don't just do their own job, but also try to do everyone else's! The 6 vibrations feel they are working too hard, and yet that hard work makes them feel indispensable. They have to learn to step back and trust that people can do their own jobs and that the work will get done. Otherwise their intense efforts can backfire, with others feeling resentful. So what I say is, "Relax, 6 Life Path, you are a powerful number and you don't have to try so hard."

NATURAL MATCH NUMBERS: *3, 6, and 9*
COMPATIBLE NUMBERS: *2, 4, and 8*
CHALLENGE NUMBERS: *1, 5, and 7*

Rosie O'Donnell is a fitting example of the 6 Life Path. Women with 6 Life Paths often feel called to be parents. This is certainly the case with Rosie O'Donnell, who has adopted several children and whose love for kids shines through her work. She has also worked tirelessly for the cause of adoption regulations, trying to make it so that more people can find children to love. At the same time, the 6 also needs to be in charge. Rosie was strong in the decision-making process of her own show and took home—can you guess it?—6 Emmys in exactly 6 years. The lawsuit concerning *Rosie* magazine was the result of her not feeling her voice could be heard in the editorial process. People were doing things without her permission, and she felt out of control, so she resigned. The 6 will not let you put words into her mouth!

Some speculated this debacle would cost Rosie her entire fortune, but she didn't listen. She insisted the truth would win out, and ultimately the judge agreed with her—deciding that the magazine was not owed any money. Rosie felt vindicated—the strength of her 6 Life Path had not let her down.

The "7" Life Path:
The Faith Seeker

There does, in fact, appear to be a plan.

—ALBERT EINSTEIN

The 7 Life Path is here to learn to have faith. If 7s don't have faith in their lives, they can't truly be happy. This doesn't necessarily mean they're going to be into organized religion—faith comes in different packages. But there is undeniably a spiritual energy surrounding the 7. If you have a 7 child, you'll notice when he or she sleeps that you seem to be looking at an angel. Luckily for those of us with 7s in our lives, they often continue to exude that beautiful spirit even when they become adults.

I honestly believe there are two kinds of people on our planet: those who thank God, and those who think they're God. This is true for the 7 more than any other number. The 7 needs a strong spiritual base. If the 7s don't believe in a higher power, or if they question the meaning of life, they'll be exhausting to have around. They will also try to escape: When they're off track, 7s, like the 5s, are drawn to drugs, alcohol, sex, travel, and overwork.

I often make the joke that 7s are just visiting the planet, because they don't seem to be *from* here. I think 7s are here observing humans, not quite sure what makes us tick. As a matter of fact, in any given year you'll find a surprising number of Oscar-nominated directors—those who turn life into art—who are 7 Life Paths. The 7 is also a great number for philosophers. It's no accident that Leonard Nimoy, who played Spock in *Star Trek*, is a 7 Life Path.

The number 7 is considered a magic number in many cultures, both ancient and modern. People who are 7s tend to have a natural psychic ability, and it's important for them to take alone time to regroup. The ability to see beyond the normal range can be a burden, but meditation can help the 7 use this ability wisely. The 7's biggest spiritual breakthroughs usually come when they are by themselves, and alone with nature. As Pythagoras said, "Those who desire wisdom should look for it in solitude."

In the Hebrew Bible—or the Old Testament—the scripture tells us that on the seventh day God rested. Mankind was then enjoined to rest on the seventh day as well. The Orthodox Jews keep very closely to this tradition—not even lighting a fire on the Sabbath.

In healthy, loving relationships, the 7 tends to be completely loyal, honest, and direct. In spite of this, Life Path 7s sometimes have trouble saying, "I love you," or praising their partner. This comes from a fear that their loved ones might realize they're too good for them and leave. The irony is that if the person does leave it's often because of feeling undervalued and neglected.

On the other hand, it's very obvious when the 7 doesn't like you because they'll tell you—and it's not a fun experience, since 7s have lethal tongues. They also have what I call a mental steel door. If 7s decide they don't want you in their lives, they'll shut that door and that'll be the end of the relationship.

The 7 loves natural beauty. Rivers, oceans, lakes—anything connected to water helps the 7 get out of his own head. This is important, since 7s tend to think too much. They also love mountains, the snow, flowers, plants, and green grass. They have a wonderful affinity for the simple things. Since they're not always good at understanding people's needs and wants, they often crave the unconditional love that comes from having pets.

The 7 is a very bright, intelligent, and intense number. Much like the Life Path 4, the 7 will overanalyze every situation. They'll walk into a room and see all of the details right away. (As a result, 7s tend to be very good writers.) They also become computer experts and scientists—anything involving technical work. Life Path 7s are good at discovering things. It would not be surprising if a 7 vibration finds the cure for AIDS. They're often able to solve difficult problems, but they may not know where the answer came from. I believe this is a result of the fact that 7s living on the positive side of their numbers are more closely linked with God than all the other Life Path Numbers.

Interestingly, 7s like to have an air of secrecy and will do anything to keep the mystery going. The more you pry or ask questions, the more the 7 shuts down. They are exclusive. Even in a marriage it's not uncommon for a 7 to sleep in a separate bed or even in a separate room. This is meant as no offense to the spouse, the 7s just need their own space. If you are in a relationship with a 7, don't take it personally when your partner becomes very quiet. The 7 needs time to assess and dissect all those thoughts and ideas.

The 7 vibrations need to work hard too. Work is their passion, and they'll throw themselves into it, because they feel like they can be in control in the working environment. Life Path 7s make good psychologists and psychiatrists—anything to do with the study of the mind. They have psychic ability, so they can excel at Numerology, astrology, and tarot card reading. They are good public speakers. They don't seek it out, it comes to them: When they speak, people want to listen to them. Other compatible occupations are those concerning the mysteries of nature: oceanography, astronomy, biology, and geology.

I also like to say that the 7 has the Peter Pan syndrome. They are children for life in many ways. Conversely, when they are children, their parents often point out that they seem like old souls. When a young 7 says something that seems beyond their years, don't disregard it: 7s have tremendous wisdom and insight, so when a 7 child tells you something, listen carefully. They have strong intuition and may see something you don't—and need to know.

The 7 can be misunderstood because often this vibration has a quality that makes people feel judged in their presence. Others may feel the 7 is cold or aloof, but I can tell you that the reason they might seem to be holding back is that they are simply observing the world.

NATURAL MATCH NUMBERS: *1, 5, and 7*
COMPATIBLE NUMBERS: *4*
CHALLENGE NUMBERS: *2, 3, 6, 8, and 9*

Mel Gibson is a case study for the 7 Life Path. We never know a 7 completely. Mel Gibson has been a superstar for years and years, yet who really knows him? We certainly know he has a huge family, but we've never seen his kids or wife in magazines, or heard his family interviewed. His private life is private, just as a 7 would insist. Moreover, Mel is a passionate Catholic—which goes right along with the spiritual 7—and was urged on by his faith to produce and direct the controversial film *The Passion of the Christ*. Rene Russo was quoted in *Entertainment Weekly* as saying, "[Mel has] always been a seeker in terms of finding God. I know our conversations were always [about] 'Where is truth? Where do you want me to go from here, God? We've been to the mountain-top—what else is there?' " These are the exact questions 7 Life Paths are always asking, and that is why Mel Gibson felt called to make this potentially risky film. (For even more about Mel's 7, see chapter 15.)

THE 7 OBSESSION

Name: Lady Diana
Soul = 1 Personality = 7 Power Name = 8

Date of birth: 7/1/1961
Birth Day = 1 Life Path = 7

Diana's Primary Numbers are: 17817 Attitude Number is: 8

Name: Marilyn Monroe
Soul = 7 Personality = 3 Power Name = 1

Date of birth: 6/1/1926
Birth Day = 1 Life Path = 7

Marilyn's Primary Numbers are: 73117 Attitude Number is: 7

The public has always been obsessed with Lady Diana and Marilyn Monroe. Let's see why. When you look at a person's Numerology chart, the Birth Day Numbers are the most significant because they cannot be changed. In this case, both women were born on a 1 Birth Day and had a 7 Life Path. In total, Diana and Marilyn had four numbers in common, which would make them very similar women in Numerology.

This is confirmed by even the most cursory look at their lives. Lady Diana was raised by a series of nannies, and by age six when her parents separated, she was sent off to boarding school. Marilyn never knew her father, and at age six was molested by someone who knew her family. From that point forward, Marilyn spent her childhood in orphanages and foster homes. These unstable early childhood beginnings made both women long for a loving environment where they could really feel that they belonged.

Interestingly, at the age of sixteen, each had a fateful introduction to her future. Marilyn got married to her first husband, and Lady Diana met her future husband, Prince Charles, for the first time. Throughout their lives both had well-publicized heartbreak in love. Marilyn married three times, and Lady Diana went through her hellish relationship with Prince Charles, who cheated on her from the beginning with Camilla Parker Bowles. Although she stayed married, she fell in love with other men and was betrayed and badly hurt by them. Both Diana and Marilyn were hungry for enduring love that forever eluded them.

When you look at their charts, you will see that both have double 1 vibrations. The negative side of this energy promotes insecurity and an inner voice that whispers, "You're not good enough." Lady Diana's severe bulimia and Marilyn Monroe's incessant drinking and pill-popping are the sort of destructive behavior patterns that are often used to quiet this negative inner voice.

Each woman died in August on a Sunday (the seventh day of the week) within three months of turning thirty-six years old. This was when they were in their prime—at the very height of their fame and beauty. Both of them died under suspicious circumstances. Lady Diana died in a car crash; Marilyn Monroe died from an overdose. The public finds ambiguity in their deaths, something not quite right. There are two theories that have stayed current concerning each woman. In Diana's case, the official story is that the driver of Lady Diana's car was intoxicated and lost control of the vehicle. Others believe her death was an assassination, and that the monarchy was horrified at the possibility that Lady Diana would marry a Muslim and compromise the queen, who is also head of the Church of England. Recently letters have been found that would seem to implicate Charles himself. None of this is substantiated, of course, but the people will not let their princess go without a fight.

In the case of Marilyn, the official story is that she either drank too much, popped too many pills or simply overdosed. At the time there was some conjecture that she had killed herself, but this seemed a pretty good time for Marilyn and her friends denied this vehemently. Theory number two is that she kept a diary about her affairs with John F. Kennedy and his brother Robert Kennedy. The Kennedy camp feared that she was so out of control in her substance abuse

that she might kiss and tell and reveal political information that was Top Secret. The only way to prevent this was to create what looked like "an accident." To this day there are new evidence and theories coming up as to the "real" killer of Monroe.

Why do we care so much? What made these two so unforgettable? It is because they are 7 Life Paths and 7s are known for their alluring sense of mystery. Other examples of famous 7 Life Paths that the public is still obsessed with are John F. Kennedy Jr. and John F. Kennedy Sr.

The public acts as though these women are alive today. Every time there is a story that comes up on Lady Diana or Marilyn Monroe, people snatch up the magazines to read the latest updates on them. This would normally seem to be very strange behavior, but from a Numerology perspective, it makes perfect sense.

The "8" Life Path:
The Executive

If you get up one more time than you fall, you will make it through.

—CHINESE PROVERB

The 8's life lesson is to establish financial security. This is not to say that 8s are materialistic. It's just that the Life Path 8 seeks the freedom that comes from being financially stable. They don't like the fact that money can be elusive, so they find ways to keep the money coming in so they'll never be without. Because of this, there are a lot of 8s who are millionaires—but who never spend a penny of it. They'd rather keep the money in the bank, where it's safe. Then there is the other kind of 8: whenever they have money, they feel the need to spend it all.

Usually 8s tend to be drawn to the finer things in life. They like quality and often have attractive possessions—a nice home, car, clothes, etc. These possessions are reminders that everything is under control financially.

The 8 has excellent executive ability, and this is also the politician's number. It's a power number, which means that while they want control, they do hope to use it to make a positive difference in the world.

The 8 is the classic workaholic. Often, a woman who is married to an 8 Life Path will get upset and tell me her husband doesn't care about her or their children. All he cares about is work. I can tell her exactly what he's thinking: "Hey, I'm trying to make things happen and achieve some goals so I can be a great provider." The same goes for 8 Life Path women; they can also get too caught up in the business world. I tell my 8 Life Path clients to remember who it is they are working so hard for! They must take time to give the people in their lives enough personal attention.

As I said above, the number 8 has a dual nature. This is evident, visually, from the numeral itself: one circle on top of the other (8). This number is sometimes interpreted as a symbol of degeneration and regeneration; when turned on its side, it becomes the symbol of infinity (∞). It's no surprise, then, that com-

plete reversals are always a possibility with this number. This can be a good thing. If an 8 has made a big decision in work or a personal relationship, and halfway through realizes it's the wrong one, it's okay to do a 180 and go the other way. That's what the 8 must learn to do instead of staying stubbornly stuck in a bad position. I often tell my 8 clients that they're allowed to change their minds.

On the other hand, the reversals can go the opposite way. The 8 Life Paths will have some difficult times in life. They may experience sorrow and wind up in circumstances where they feel humiliated. An example of just this sort of reversal is Martha Stewart. She worked hard, amassed a great fortune, and then one bad move toppled it all. It's no surprise that the bad decision was about money—it didn't matter that she stood to lose just a fraction of her overall fortune; as an 8 Life Path she couldn't bear the thought of financial loss, no matter how small.

Life Path 8s tend to be huge successes or major failures—often both in one lifetime. The 8s just need to keep their focus on any endeavor they pursue, and they will experience success. That said, 8s should remember it's important to stop and smell the roses.

It is common for an 8 Life Path to be misinterpreted by others. To avoid this, the 8 must learn to be more tactful. They tend to tell the truth about what they're thinking, neglecting to edit their remarks for the larger audience. Often they'll say something and have the other person respond with shock at how hurtful the remark was. At that point it's the 8's turn to be stunned: All they did was tell the truth. This is a very black-and-white vibration, with little room for gray areas. What I remind the 8 is that very few of us can handle the cold, harsh truth without at least a gentle preamble. It's an art form that every Life Path should perfect, especially the 8. You can still say what you feel, just be careful how you say it.

The 8 Life Path considers strife and struggle to be a normal part of life, but the one thing an 8 cannot get over is infidelity. If a partner cheats on an 8, it is best for the 8 to let that person go. It would take a supernatural effort for the 8 to get over it. Even if they stay with the partner, the 8 will never really be able to forgive them.

The 8 Life Path does not have much tolerance for people who feel sorry for themselves. An 8 who sees someone suffer will likely say, "Look, I'm sorry that happened to you. Now get up." This is ironic, since 8s often see themselves as a victim. That's because 8 Life Paths don't get away with much in this world. If an 8 Life Path were driving five miles per hour over the speed limit and another Life Path was going twice that, the 8 would get the ticket. It's part of the reality of being an 8. The key is getting through it without taking on a "woe is me" attitude. I recommend humor to my clients. Learn to laugh at life! Rent a funny movie and surround yourself with amusing people. Even listening to music that makes you happy can help you relax and let go—disco, jazz, whatever sets you free. Remember, these hardships are usually temporary. Life is not as overwhelming as you think. Dwelling on the negative, especially if you're an 8, can lead to a deep depression. I want to keep you healthy, so I encourage you to learn to laugh as much as possible.

A good piece of news is that 8s are late bloomers. If you're an 8 Life Path and you're thinking, Gosh, I wonder if I'm too old to do what I want to do, I'm here to say you are never too old. As long as you're on this planet, you can make your dreams come true.

I do caution 8s about their health. It is not hard for them to get hurt, so they must be on the alert when driving and playing sports. Paying attention to the moment can make all the difference—I think many 8s get so caught up in their work and dreams that they don't always pay attention to the simple things that cause physical stress and trouble.

Occupations that suit the 8 include banker, stock market trader, accountant, office manager, and engineer. This Life Path also makes good corporate lawyers or judges. Many 8s go into the field of wedding planning, interior decorating and/or running nonprofit organizations. They are often physically beautiful, so modeling and acting are common career pursuits as well. Big business is a natural for the 8, like running a network or a major publishing company. If the Life Path 8 has a 3, 6 or 9 in their birth numbers, then their professions may lean toward the creative arts, perhaps in areas of live performance. Now, if you have a dream that is very different than what I've listed here, go for it! This is your life and you need to seize the moment. Keep in mind that "life is not a dress rehearsal." Today is a gift. As an 8 you are always planning for the future. The future may never come! Today is what you've got; embrace it.

NATURAL MATCH NUMBERS: *2, 4, and 8*
COMPATIBLE NUMBERS: *5 (in business), 6*
CHALLENGE NUMBERS: *1, 3, 7, and 9*

Note: Although the 8 falls in the Natural Match category, it can feel like a Challenge Number to a fellow 8 Vibration.

Cindy Crawford is a beautiful 8 Life Path woman who has turned her assets into a remarkable career. Life Path 8s care about their physical appearance, and Cindy has gone so far as to make beauty into her life's work. But Cindy also has a killer business instinct that has meant solid financial security for her and those she loves. This is the key to the 8's motivation. In a business that can chew you up and spit you out, Cindy has persevered for over two decades. At age thirty-seven and after giving birth to two children, she's still going strong. She's undertaken countless spokeswoman contracts, has tried her hand at acting, has produced successful workout videos, and has even written a children's book. She's ventured into practically every notable entertainment field to continue marketing the Cindy Crawford brand. As family is really the center of the 8's world, it's no surprise that when Cindy's younger brother died of cancer, she felt called to crusade for children with the disease. She will continue to evolve as a person, and will always find new ways to do well in business, help others, and make the world a better place.

The "9" Life Path:
The Humanitarian

The positive thinker sees the invisible, feels the intangible, and achieves the impossible.

—ANONYMOUS

The 9 is the most evolved number in Numerology, and is considered one of the strongest of all the Vibrations because it contains the qualities of all the other numbers. When a 9 has a strong spiritual base, they are a wonderful source of light in the world. Indeed, there is a selfless quality to the 9. It's also the highest of the single vibrations and is ruled by determination. This Life Path has a strong inclination to follow something believed in, and they will pursue it with tremendous ambition and drive. As a result, there will always be people who are jealous and resentful of the 9. I suggest that the 9s follow the old adage: "Keep your friends close, and your enemies closer." The 9 needs to be aware of those trying to sabotage their plans, and make an effort to put this kind of person at ease. Some people will see you as condescending and you need to be aware of this fact before you speak.

It is really upsetting to the 9 Life Path to work hard for something and then it doesn't come to fruition. The 9s have an authentic regard for humanity, so their goals usually serve others well. When 9s fail, they feel they've failed the world. One of the strongest characteristics of 9 Life Paths is that they often have issues with their original family. They may feel unloved or abandoned by their mother or father, or they may feel completely responsible for their parents. Either way, the 9's attachment to her original family is hard to give up.

When they marry and start their own family, 9s want nothing less than to be the "perfect parent." Of course there is no such thing as a perfect parent— or a perfect child. Children come through us, but we do not own them. They are here to teach us something, and we are here to teach them. I say 9s need to go easy on themselves and not take life so hard, lest they feel like failures when something goes wrong with their kids—which we all know will happen at some point or another.

When it comes to the family, the 9 cannot handle interference. If having trouble with their partners, they don't want their parents or siblings to get involved. The 9 feels capable of resolving the situation—and since the 9 is the number of completion, that's probably right. The answers come to 9 Life Paths when they engage their spiritual side and listen to the inner voice.

The 9 Life Paths do so much and take such good care of everybody's business that when they are in trouble, people don't even notice. People look at a 9 and think: Oh, he's so strong, he doesn't need *my* help. I always tell 9s to let their guards down a bit more, to ask for a hug or a kiss when they need one. They're not a Life Path whose needs are easily read by others—they have to ask.

The 9s don't need to be the center of attention, but people put them there anyway. If a 9 Vibration is standing in a department store, everyone assumes that person works there. If a 9 walks into a classroom, people ask, "Are you the teacher?" They just assume the 9 is in charge, and that's why the 9 *should* be in charge—because 9s don't abuse the privilege. They are not rude to those who are under their authority. No matter what they set their minds on, or whether they've ever done it before, the 9 will manage to pull it off. Things just seem to work out for the 9. Ironically, 9 Life Paths are the only ones who don't see this! They're very hard on themselves, and even if they do a good job, they will beat themselves up if it wasn't perfect. I think 9s need to lighten up and forgive themselves for being human.

There is, on the other hand, a really intimidating quality to the 9. Sometimes people will be jealous of or competitive with the 9, yet the 9s compete with no one. They are simply doing the best they can. I believe it's actually the 9's job to put others at ease. It's as simple as the 9 remembering to say, "Hey, I really like your haircut," or, "Gee, what a nice suit." These simple words will disarm people who would otherwise see the 9 as an enemy.

The 9 Life Path is often accused of being patronizing. They may not think that they know everything, but others view them as feeling that way. This breeds resentment and competition in those around the 9 vibration. It's a hard lesson to learn, but 9s must understand that on some subconscious level people can feel the 9 is on a higher vibration. The 9 Life Paths must remind themselves, "Forgive them, for they know not what they do."

If a 9 does something good, people follow. If a 9 does something bad, people also follow. They make amazing teachers, school counselors, and therapists. They're really good with children, and children tend to love them. They're excellent doctors, nurses, and social workers. They do well in creative fields as lecturers, artists, illustrators, and writers, and perform as musicians and actors.

My most important piece of advice for 9 Life Paths is to take care not to live in the past. When they get into the moment, they can make a positive difference in this world—and that, after all, is what the 9 is here to do.

NATURAL MATCH NUMBERS: *3, 6, and 9*
COMPATIBLE NUMBERS: *1, 2, and 5*
CHALLENGE NUMBERS: *4, 7, and 8*

Mahatma Gandhi is the ultimate example of the 9 Life Path. Gandhi was the greatest humanitarian India has ever known, and did whatever it took to liberate his countrymen and bring peace to the nation he loved. He put this goal above all else, including his physical health—starving himself nearly to death in protest on more than one occasion. The people loved him so much that they were willing to put down their arms to keep him from death. He truly believed that nonviolence was the way to freedom, and without firing a shot managed to free the entire subcontinent of India from British rule. One of his most famous quotations is: "Peace will not come out of the clash of arms, but out of justice lived and done by unarmed nations in the face of odds." This is exactly the mindset of the healthy 9 Life Path. Gandhi was a man who lived in the moment, never letting yesterday or tomorrow get in the way of his mission; he was and will always be an inspiring example of the compassionate 9 Life Path.

Our Life Path numbers have much to teach us. They show us our strengths, as well as our potential weaknesses. But what if you read your description and thought, That doesn't really sound like me? Does that mean Numerology is not for you?

Absolutely not. You must keep in mind that there are four other numbers, plus the Attitude Number. Taking a close look at your Soul Number, Personality Number, Power Name Number, and Birth Day Number will help you understand any perceived inconsistencies with your Life Path Number. That's the focus of chapters 5, 6, 7, and 8, the other four numbers that make up the five Primary Numbers; and the Attitude Number is found in chapter 9.

Four

Healing by the Numbers

▪ HEALING THROUGH AFFIRMATIONS ▪

At this point I would like to talk about affirmations because I think they can help make your life what you want it to be. Affirmations are an effective way to reprogram your mind. When you have a habitual negative thought, it will pop into your head no less than 400 times a day. Replace this with a positive affirmation at least that many times—which is a minimum of fifteen to twenty minutes a day. Affirmations are positive statements you repeat to yourself, either silently or out loud, that help release you from negative beliefs and habitual patterns. They are our way of telling the universe what we want and need, and manifesting the best possible future for ourselves.

If you haven't seen the power of affirmations in your life yet, you might be skeptical that they work. But just try using the affirmations in this book—I've seen thousands of my clients reap their benefits, so I know they can and will work for you. You can do five minutes in the morning, ten at night, if that's what it takes to work in your fifteen minutes a day. These are affirmations tailored to your numbers.

I've gotten to the point of starting off the day using affirmations before I even open my eyes in the morning. How long before it becomes a habit? Thirty days. You can begin by focusing on the affirmations listed for your Life Path. Later, pick the one(s) you need at that moment about whatever is making you insecure: money, love, or lack of self-confidence.

A healthy 1 is independent, self-motivated, a hard worker.

The 1 Life Path is so critical of themselves, they can be critical of other people. Their competitiveness can lead to their feeling empty. They have to keep moving and they have a hard time embracing the moment.

They have such a need to be in first place that literally anybody who offers advice or tries to tell them how to live their life makes them defensive and angry. They feel someone is trying to be better than they are or someone is trying to make them feel less. This is all inner turmoil that they have to work out.

If your Life Path is a 1, here's an affirmation if you find yourself living in the negative side of your 1 Life Path: To combat that critical bully in yourself, affirm, fifteen to twenty minutes every day: **"I recognize the miracle of my being. I am enough."** Stand in front of the mirror and gaze into your eyes. At first you will feel foolish, but eventually you will be more accepting of yourself. By doing this often, other people will be kinder to you as well.

"I am perfectly content to be me. I am good enough just as I am."

A healthy 2 is harmonious, loving, and a peacemaker.

The downside of a 2 Life Path is that they feel they've given so much, they might end up *whining* and saying, "Oh, I've done so much for so many people!" Or they get so angry, because they're easygoing, that when they finally lose it, it's overwhelming and they simply look like the terrible 2, a spoiled child.

Here's an affirmation if you find yourself on the negative side of your 2 Life Path:

"I am the calm expression of peace and see the love in everybody."

A healthy 3 is upbeat, enthusiastic, and optimistic about themselves and others.

The creative 3 Life Path doesn't do well with the standard nine-to-five job. If stuck, they can create some pretty wild drama in their life. They make up stories and exaggerate the truth, because they don't want life to be run of the mill. They have to use their creative gifts. They can seem manic-depressive, experiencing violent mood swings if they're not using their talents.

The phrase "All the world's a stage" is really true for a 3. Because so many 3s wind up in some form of entertainment, here is an excellent affirmation regarding that dream. If indeed it is your dream to be famous and successful, a great affirmation would be:

"I welcome my fame and fortune today."

You start affirming: "I welcome my fame and fortune today. . . . I welcome my fame and fortune today. . . . I welcome my fame and fortune today." You could do this in your car or maybe when you're at home and you have time. Eventually you're going to give your subconscious permission to have it today. Not tomorrow. Today.

When I was performing as a comedienne, I always affirmed, **"I love my audience and my audience loves me."** After a show, people inevitably would run up to me and say, "I love you, Glynis." And I would think, Of course you do, *dahling,* I affirmed it. You never had a choice.

Here's another affirmation if you find yourself on the negative side of your 3 Life Path:

"I trust the process of life, and in the movies of my mind, I am loved and at peace."

A recurring lack or problem in your life comes from negative feedback in your subconscious. The affirmations can do a great deal to turn this around.

A healthy 4 would be seeking knowledge, providing security, and sharing expertise through teaching.

The downside of the 4 Life Path is that they plan too much for the future. They're so busy deciding what they're going to do thirteen years from now when they have a certain amount of money, or whatever their plan is, that they forget to do their living now. They exist in their own heads too much and people feel alone in their presence.

Here's an affirmation if you find yourself on the negative side of your 4 Life Path:

"I do not fear the future. Today is my most precious gift, and I am safe."

Also, 4s are famous for saying, "I don't like to argue," but then they wind up in arguments. If that's true for you, try this affirmation:

"I speak with kindness and love. I look for the good in everybody."

A healthy 5 celebrates life, and is adventurous and passionate.

The downside of a 5 Life Path: They tend to create drama because they have a fear that life won't be exciting. They also abuse drugs, alcohol, food, and sex. They have to be careful not to go into overkill, not to overdo. They have to use their passionate energy in a healthy way.

The 5's affirmation would be:

"I'm willing to change the thoughts that created this condition."

Or you could affirm:

"I easily ask for what I need. Life supports me completely."

The healthy 6 seeks harmony, is nurturing and wise.

Because the 6 Life Path is a number that rescues other people, they can be overbearing. The 6 can try to control everyone to make sure everything's handled.

When things are going too well they panic and say, "Oh, gosh, it's going too smoothly, it's too good to be true," and then things fall apart. The 6 often thinks they could do better alone, but when left alone, they wish they weren't.

Use the affirmation we talk about in conjunction with Finding Your Perfect Mate.

"I welcome a loving, nurturing relationship with a man (or woman) who will be emotionally available to me, who will be honest, passionate, and funny, who will be my equal, and my life partner."

When you are doing that affirmation, regardless of whatever your energy is, you should include whatever your hangup is. If you need a lot of money because wealth matters to you, it should also say:

". . . a man (or woman) . . . who is well to do."

Or if you've had partners who have cheated on you, then add the word *faithful* to that affirmation.

A 6 Life Path often puts people on a pedestal. Eventually the person will fall down, and the 6 will let them know it. One affirmation to help end this pattern is:

"I see with eyes of love. There's a harmonious solution and I accept it now."

A healthy 7 is intelligent. They have a gentle spirit and intuition.

Because they have a loner quality, 7s don't need people, and they often have communication breakdowns. The 7 Life Path escapes through, sex, alcohol, food, drugs, geography—anything they can think of. That's the downside of the 7.

Try affirming:

"I breathe in life freely and trust the flow and process of life."

Another affirmation would be:

"Divine right action is taking place at all times."

A healthy 8 is ambitious, has a head for business, and real executive ability.

Because they're here to master money, the downside of the 8 Life Path is going to be one of two things: Either they become so greedy there's never enough money, or they're so afraid they're going to lose the money that it is all in the bank, that when they die it's still in the bank. Money should flow like the ocean; it comes and goes freely. The 8 can become so preoccupied with making money that they become workaholics and the family can feel neglected.

A good affirmation would be:

"I believe in infinite abundance and the money is always there."

When someone betrays an 8 Life Path, it is difficult for the 8 to let it go. This hatred has a boomerang effect and causes the 8 even more pain. Here is an affirmation to help heal this problem:

"Each day I live in the moment, by forgiving those in my past."

A healthy 9 has compassion for others and is a dynamic leader.

The 9 Life Path can stay stuck in their past, talking about what their mother or father did wrong. In my Numerology practice, I have found a disproportionate number of 9s who are adopted, or have lost a parent at an early age. They have a hard time letting go of their past. Because they're so busy taking care of everybody, they wind up feeling that no one cares about them. They miss the fact that people do love them and want to help if they would just let them.

Try this affirmation:

"I joyfully release all of the past and let only love surround me."

▪ HEALING YOUR PHYSICAL BODY BY THE NUMBERS ▪

I am a firm believer that what we do not deal with mentally will eventually attack us physically. So it's no surprise that throughout my career as a Numerologist, I have seen specific health problems occur over and over in certain Life Path Numbers.

Moreover, many of today's most revered spiritual thinkers recommend the use of affirmations to help cure physical illness. Deepak Chopra, Louise L. Hay, Shakti Gawain, and many others recognize that most diseases do not begin in the body, but in the mind and spirit. By the time the body has been attacked by the illness, the person had been suffering emotionally, mentally, or spiritually for a long time. The actual physical manifestation is the way the body reacts to what is troubling the person's spirit. Luckily, there is a way to avoid and help heal physical ailments: the use of affirmations.

▪ THE POWER OF NUMBERS ▪

Healing by the numbers truly works—here's something that happened to me. Years ago, when I was doing standup comedy, I was in a close business relationship where the two main people I had to deal with had Life Paths that were Toxic to mine. During that time, I was constantly losing my voice and getting laryngitis. Quite by chance, I picked up a book on healing your body through affirmations. I read that losing my voice meant I had swallowed anger and did not feel I was, or could be, heard. If your voice isn't being heard, what's the use of speaking? As a 3 Life Path who was actually making a living through my voice, you can imagine how frightening this was for me. I started to repeat the following affirmation fifteen minutes a day:

"What I say does matter. I am heard and I do make a difference.
Love is all around me."

When I would get a laryngitis attack it would normally take me five or six days to get my voice back. But after repeating my affirmation over and over, my voice came back within a day.

The next time I had laryngitis, I woke up at 9:00 A.M. and I had a radio interview scheduled for noon. My voice was completely gone, not even a croak or a whisper. I had some faith in the affirmation system by now but I was still frightened—I only had three hours! I picked a peaceful place, lit a white candle to further focus my energies, and whispered the affirmation for one hour. At 11:00 A.M. I decided to try speaking out loud. To my absolute delight, my voice was completely back. That's all it took to convince me that affirmations work. I started reciting my affirmations daily, even when I was in good voice. Almost fifteen years later, I can truthfully say that I have not lost my voice since—no matter what circumstances I have found myself in. I've also used different affirmations for different ailments I've encountered, and my experience is that they have worked every time.

▪ AFFIRMATIONS BY LIFE PATH AND DIS-EASE ▪

I once read a book called *The Three-Pound Universe*—the title refers to the weight of the human brain. When you reprogram your brain, you have a whole new Universe to live in—and that's where the healing begins. We all play negative dialogues over and over in our minds; the only way to reprogram the subconscious and reverse the messages we've been giving ourselves for so long is to repeat a positive, healing affirmation over and over for no less than fifteen minutes a day. The results are well worth the effort.

I have prepared a list of health problems that affect certain Life Path Numbers, and I have put them into Natural Match categories. The particular diseases that are listed for each set are especially likely to manifest themselves in people with the Life Path vibrations listed. As you read about each medical problem, you will notice that the description of the disease resembles the Life Path in that particular Natural Match category. For example, the 6 Life Path is the natural parent. The breast, a symbol of parenting, is often the target of disease in a 6; you wouldn't believe the number of 6 women I've met who have had breast cancer or a breast cancer scare. Similarly, 4s want control above all else—consequently, they often suffer panic attacks and anxiety when they feel they're not in the driver's seat. The 2 Life Path is very sensitive and can suffer from diseases of the heart. Many of my 2 clients have heart trouble, and whenever I hear that someone has died of a "broken heart" my first thought is that the person must have been a 2 Life Path.

My goal in this chapter is to help you heal yourselves by the numbers, so after each ailment I will give you an affirmation to perform. In order to get results, you need to use these affirmations on a daily basis. Carve out at least fifteen minutes, find a quiet corner, and remind your family not to bother you. Then repeat the affirmation over and over to yourself, paying attention to the words.

If you find one of your physical ailments is not listed as a Natural Match for your Life Path vibration, by all means find the disease under another number and do the affirmation I've supplied. You have five Primary Numbers, plus Attitude and Destiny Numbers, and your "dis-ease" could be coming from one of your other vibrations crying out.

Please remember that I am not a doctor, and that the affirmations I offer are not meant to replace the care of your physician. If you are suffering any of the ailments listed and have not yet consulted your physician, put down this book right now, pick up the phone, and call for an appointment.

For those of you who have already been diagnosed, I suggest you do the affirmation for your particular ailment and see the difference it makes. Also, if there is a hereditary dis-ease in your family that you are afraid of getting (heart disease, breast cancer, obesity, etc.), start doing the affirmation for that illness as a preventive.

Natural Match Category 1, 5, 7

AILMENT	POSSIBLE ORIGIN	AFFIRMATION
Alcoholism	A feeling of hopelessness, desire to escape from reality	I embrace reality. I need the world and the world needs me.
Arthritis	Hypercritical of others and ourselves	I am fine as I am, and life is good. I release all negativity.
Hair Loss	This is a sign of too much tension in the scalp; overcontrolling	I believe in the wisdom of life. I can relax and I am cared for.

AILMENT	POSSIBLE ORIGIN	AFFIRMATION
Hemorrhoids	Feeling incapable, rushed, burdened by unfinished business	There is time enough to do what I must, and I am always on time.
Hives	Hidden fears and dilemmas, tendency to make too much of nothing	I am whole and at peace in my calm center, and nothing touches this.
Infections	Irritations have gotten to you	I have at my center an unchanging place of endless peace.
Insomnia	Fear of the natural cycles of life	I embrace the peace and healing of sleep, with no fear of tomorrow.
Knee Troubles	Inability to flow with life's changes and issues	I am always ready to reason with and understand others. I am loved as I continue to change.
Middle Back Pain	The burden of old guilt and regrets	I am free of the past and all its burdens—I move forward from this time.
Mouth Problems	Resistance to accepting new ideas and situations	I am nourished by the good that comes to me in healthful abundance.
Neck Problems	Being inflexible on issues, having difficulty seeing other sides of a dispute	I treat others fairly and I respect their ideas and attract people who respect mine.
Night Blindness	Fear of the dark, new situations, or unfamiliar territory	I am one with life and the universe. Wherever I go, I am always home.
Tooth Problems	Troubles with family, indecision in life situations	My decisions are guided by divine inspiration and the wisdom of the universe.
Ulcers	Something is gnawing at you	I am strong and nothing can pierce my peaceful self.

Natural Match Category 2, 4, 8

AILMENT	POSSIBLE ORIGIN	AFFIRMATION
Allergies	Failure to identify what truly bothers you; feeling of separateness	I am one with the universe, and the universe will keep me safe.
Asthma	A sense of being smothered, feeling unable to breathe in your environment	I am here to joyously live my life; I will survive and I will thrive.
Back Trouble (overall)	A belief that we are unsupported in our lives	I am strong in my life's path, and always find the help I need.
Bad Breath (chronic)	Bad words, gossip, old negative thinking	I breathe in and out with love and kindness.
Constipation	Failure to rid ourselves of concepts that are no longer needed	I release the old and useless and welcome what's new and vital.
Eye Trouble	Desire to avoid what you see around you	I clearly see the good in this beautiful world.
Headaches	Believing you are unimportant, and that your needs will not be met	I accept with joy my place in the universe and know my needs are met.
High and Low Blood Pressure	High blood pressure is the boiling up of unresolved issues; low blood pressure is a feeling of hopelessness in regard to problems	There is a solution to every problem and I have the power to use it.
Lower Back	Fear of financial lack or failure	I am one with the universe, which is bountiful and supplies all that I need.
Lung Problems	A resistance to the acceptance of life	Life is good and I take it in without fear.
Panic Attacks	Fear of the unknown, and of losing control	I always have all the help I need at all times and in every situation.

| Shaky Hands | Unwillingness to grasp problems, tendency to "drop the ball" | I take life joyfully into my hands, and I know I will succeed. |
| Skin Trouble | Skin is our armor, and problems come from a belief that our armor is not protecting us | I am whole and safe within my being and nothing negative can enter here. |

Natural Match Category 3, 6, 9

AILMENT	POSSIBLE ORIGIN	AFFIRMATION
Athlete's Foot	Irritation with one's path in life	I enjoy my journey, and I can safely move on.
Breast Cysts	Overmothering those we love, and trying to control every situation	I lovingly release the ones who love me, and I give them freedom to live their lives, as I am free to live mine.
Diabetes	Need for a kinder, sweeter existence; a longing for balance	Today, I have all I need for perfect harmony in body and spirit.
Earaches	Shutting out the world and only hearing the negative	I accept the beautiful sounds of the world without pain or fear.
Indigestion	Fear and anxiety, excess complaining	Life comes to me in beautiful waves of peace and calm.
Menstrual Trouble	Not accepting fully the power of feminine sexuality	I love my body, I am proud to be a woman.
Migraine Headaches	Feeling that others are controlling you; no choices of your own. Belief that you need to be sick to rest	I am the director of my life, and it is okay for me to rest when I need to.
Overeating	Fear of being in want, substituting food for love	I will always have enough to eat, and I love and am loved in return.
Shoulder Pain	Feeling overburdened	I accept my responsibilities with joy and know I can carry them well.

AILMENT	POSSIBLE ORIGIN	AFFIRMATION
Stomach Trouble	Resistance to new ideas; fear of change	I welcome the new, and embrace the future. I am where I should be at all times.
Throat Trouble (Laryngitis)	Fear of speaking up, unexpressed anger, unappreciated creativity	I have a right to be heard, my ideas are important and always for the highest good.
Tumors	Hanging on to old hurts and issues; allowing guilt to grow inside	The past is gone and I am happy on this day, completely forgiven and embraced by life.
Upper Back Pain	Believing one is not loved and not wanting to share love	I am loved and supported by life.
Urinary Tract Infection	Angry at intimates, especially those of the opposite sex	I release you from my expectations, and live in perfect harmony with others and myself.

▪ CANCER, HEART ATTACKS, AND EATING DISORDERS ▪

These three major diseases are in a special category. After doing thousands of readings, I have discovered that all Life Paths are susceptible to these ailments. Often, however, the diseases manifest themselves in different Life Paths for different reasons. I've listed some examples below, as well as affirmations that are appropriate for all nine Life Paths suffering from these disorders.

Cancers

Life Path 2s internalize all of their problems and this negative turmoil can result in unexplainable cancer. The 5 Life Path may develop a cancerous tumor in the brain because he or she can't stop thinking. They may start to believe that the "computer in the mind" is defective, and suddenly a tumor develops to validate this belief.

An affirmation for all Life Paths to help prevent or overcome cancers:

"I affirm the complete perfection of the universe, I am a child of the universe and I live in perfect love and joy."

Heart Attacks

The 1 Life Path may get heart attacks because they never stop moving. They may let their health deteriorate as a result. The 8 Life Path might have a heart attack because they are so focused on work, they have difficulty listening to anyone, let alone their own bodies.

An affirmation for all Life Paths to help prevent or overcome heart problems:

"My heart beats with the rhythm of life itself. It is growing stronger every day."

Anorexia/Bulimia/Overeating

The 2 Life Path may develop anorexia/bulimia because they feel unattractive and need to be in control of their appearance on some level. A 6 Life Path overeater may feel so overburdened by needing to take care of others that he or she gains weight to keep the world at bay. I have often said that a 6 Life Path tries to take care of everyone on the planet, and must be careful not to become "the size of the planet."

An affirmation for all charts to help prevent or overcome an eating disorder:

"I love myself and I welcome life-giving nourishment for my body from the endless abundance of life."

Five

The Soul Number

As I have stated throughout this book, the basic definition of each number does not change; it's the *placement* of the number that changes. The placement of the number also determines the level of the number's importance. The Life Path Number is the most important number in your chart, but the Soul Number is necessary to understand because it is what you *feel inside*. Your Soul Number may not come across to those who meet you. They may see more extroverted numbers, like your Power Name Number. But you must fully understand what is vibrating in your soul, because that's the number that will lead you to inner peace.

▪ WHAT IS THE SOUL NUMBER? ▪

When you add all the vowels in your name and break it down to one digit, you will get your soul number. (Refer to the Pythagorean Number System found on page 11.) Here are two examples:

$$3 + \quad 9 + \quad 9 + \quad 5 + \quad 1 + 5 = 32 = 3 + 2 = 5$$

JUSTIN TIMBERLAKE

Soul Number = 5

Justin has a 5 Soul Number. This tells me that his soul is fulfilled when he is unrestricted; he will be happiest when he's free to look for new excitement.

$$9 + \quad 5 + \quad 5+1 = 20 = 2 + 0 = 2$$

BRITNEY SPEARS

Soul Number = 2

Britney has a 2 Soul Number. Her soul needs constant reassurance that she is loved and very special. If the person she loves is unavailable to her, this would cause her emotional distress.

Since a 5 and a 2 Soul Number are considered a Challenge to each other, it could easily cause miscommunication, and in this case sadly ended the relationship.

▪ SOUL NUMBER DEFINITIONS ▪

The Soul Number is a subtle number—we do not always see its traits outwardly expressed in ourselves and others. If we are living contrary to our Soul Number, however, we will see it expressed through unhappiness and a feeling that we are unfulfilled. This is why it's so important to study the Soul Number.

The 1 Soul Number

My 1 soul is fulfilled when I have a personal victory or feel I have just won some sort of competition. When I feel I am number one at what I do, and I am treated with respect. When I have the courage to just be me, and feel completely accepted.

The 2 Soul Number

My 2 soul is fulfilled when I am in love, and have found myself in a harmonious environment; when I use my powerful intuition and solve the problem at hand; when I hear my favorite music and bring good people together.

The 3 Soul Number

My 3 soul is fulfilled when I am laughing, performing, writing, or using my creativity in a significant way; when I am giving good advice to someone and they use it.

The 4 Soul Number

My 4 soul is fulfilled when I have security, and all my bills are paid. When I have a solid plan for the future and I live in an environment that I can truly call my home. When I can share knowledge with others and I know they benefit from my expertise.

The 5 Soul Number

My 5 soul is fulfilled when I have the freedom to come and go as I please; when I can travel and uncover all the mysteries of the world; when I am at an amazing restaurant, hotel, or party celebrating life.

The 6 Soul Number

My 6 soul is fulfilled when I have children. When I run my own company and I have a lot of responsibility. When people look up to me and acknowledge all of my hard work. When I am needed and appreciated by the people in my life.

The 7 Soul Number

My 7 soul is fulfilled when I can be alone with my thoughts and surrounded by nature's beauty—the ocean, mountains, and the redwoods; when I have found a spiritual base that I can truly believe in.

The 8 Soul Number

My 8 soul is fulfilled when I have financial freedom, job security, and a nice home. When I am in charge and people do as I say. When I speak the truth and see justice in a difficult situation.

The 9 Soul Number

My 9 soul is fulfilled when I have resolved old family issues that have caused me pain. When I am living in the moment taking in everything that life has to offer me. When I am making a good living and it involves contributing to humanity.

If your Soul Number is a Natural Match to your Life Path Number, then just concentrate on fulfilling your Life Path Number, and your soul will be content as well. If your Soul Number is a Challenge Number to your Life Path, then it will require some extra work on your part. One of my 4 Life Path clients has a 3 in his soul. He is an engineer and works on a computer all day long. When I saw the 3 in his soul, I asked him what he liked to do that was creative. He said that he used to play guitar but stopped because his life got too busy. I was not surprised to learn he was dissatisfied, because he was in fact neglecting his Soul Number.

I told him he needed to start playing his guitar again and it would change his entire outlook. He started playing approximately six hours a week, and when I saw him the next time, he was glowing! He told me he had recently played his guitar at the local coffee shop and delighted all the patrons there. His wife couldn't get over the change in his disposition, and said that she had no idea he would *even enjoy* performing. She could only see him as a solid, predictable 4. She did not know there was a spontaneous 3 inside him dying to express itself.

I think of the Soul Number as "The Secret Number" because you will not always see the traits on the exterior of the person. The exception would be if the Soul Number is found in other parts of a person's chart. *Any time a number repeats itself, it becomes more obvious in a person.* To learn more about repeating numbers, refer to chapter 10.

Let's say you have a met a person who is a 1 Life Path. This person is working all the time, and appears to be very independent. However, you find your new friend has a 2 Soul Number, and will never feel complete without love. If you are looking for a possible life partner, you will not feel as threatened by his or her independence, because you understand that this person is very capable of being a life partner.

Knowing and understanding your partner's Soul Number as well as your own can only enhance the relationship. As you can see, Numerology has many layers. Keep it simple, and it will only change your life for the better!

Six

The Personality Number

What is a Personality Number? When you add all the consonants of your name together you will get your Personality Number. This number tells you how you appear on the outside, that is to say, how the world sees you.

Here's an example:

K O B E B R Y A N T

2+   2+   2+9+7+   5+2

= 29 = 2 + 9 = 11 = 1 + 1 = 2

Add the consonants straight across, breaking them down to one digit.

Kobe Bryant appears as a 2, which is his Personality Number. The 2 represents love and gentleness. That would explain why America fell madly in love with him and saw him as a basketball hero. Well, his Life Path is a 5 and that is a Challenge to his 2 Personality Number. When your Personality Number is a

Challenge to your Life Path Number, you do not appear as you really are. The 5s often find themselves in the buffet of life when it comes to sexual variety, and because the 2 is so sensual, it can be hard to resist temptation.

▪ PERSONALITY NUMBER DESCRIPTIONS ▪

The 1 Personality: People see the 1 Personality as independent, self-motivated, someone who's going places. The number 1 embodies action, strength, and power. It's in your every move, and I am reminded of the words from a wonderful old song, "Will everyone here kindly step to the rear, and let a winner lead the way." It is not that you think you are better than everyone else, but you *must* take the lead. It's your birthright. Fortunately, the world is usually willing to see that you are in the power seat. You often start trends, and you can be depended on to lead community projects, and skillfully delegate tasks to get the job done. The prestige that comes with leadership makes it all worth it to you. You would do well to be self-employed; 1s don't enjoy taking orders. Well-meaning advice can be valuable, so try to be more open to suggestions.

The 2 Personality: The 2 Personality appears as someone who is the peacemaker, the born mediator. You do best in partnerships. You have to watch being oversensitive, and learn to establish boundaries, for you are a person who appears to be the perfect friend, and some, not so worthy, would take advantage of this. The 2 Personality feels incomplete alone, and even avoids the spotlight, seeking companionship above all else. This number favors marriage and business alliances. Your innate fairness and sincerity give you a good chance of succeeding at both.

The 3 Personality: As a 3 you love dressing up. Your appearance is important to you. You're happy when you're well groomed and prepared to greet your public. Your gift is communication. The 3 Personality is someone who is witty and fun to be around. You love to give advice, and even if it's unsolicited, it's usually well received. You are a good listener (and an even better talker), and you love the telephone. In fact, conversation is a huge part of your life. But work on your mood swings; even though you snap right out of it, others don't always get over them as quickly. Bringing joy to others is what really fulfills you.

The 4 Personality: The 4 Personality appears as someone who is serious-minded, sensitive, and intelligent. You are always open to learning something new. However, if you think you are right about something, you will not give up your position. People know they can count on you to get a job done. You are usually carefully groomed and have an efficient aura, the perfect businessman or woman. Your need to impart knowledge sometimes gives people the impression that you are "raining on their parade." That is not your intention, but you might consider this when others are sometimes inexplicably annoyed with you. When this happens, let them know what you really mean.

The 5 Personality: The 5 Personality has an air of fun and energy that makes you a welcome addition to any party, and the 5 Personality is someone who wants to know where the party is! You are very clever and others enthuse to your ideas. The 5s love excitement and seek adventure, and failing that—gossip, someone else's adventure! Watch overindulgence; you can have an addictive streak. Unfortunately, you can become easily bored. Try to find harmless things to refuel your interest—sports, movies, and books are some suggestions.

The 6 Personality: The 6 Personality appears as kind and responsible—someone who takes good care of others—a born nurturer. People feel safe around you and you often find yourself in the role of "parent." The employees of a 6 will feel taken care of. You tend to spoil the people you love. Try not to do this, because if they are not grateful, you will resent them. They can depend on the 6's stability. The 6 personality is charismatic. The 6 never goes unnoticed, and people are drawn to you.

The 7 Personality: The 7 Personality appears as someone who needs privacy. You often keep to yourself, but you are an acute observer of the human scene. When you share knowledge you tend to speak with authority and you have a good memory for detail. People sometimes think that your silence means you are not listening, but the 7 is always tuned in. People feel your spirituality, which is a large part of you, and while you do not seek them out, they often come to you.

The 8 Personality: The 8 Personality appears as someone who is strong and disciplined. They carry themselves with innate dignity. The 8 has definite opinions about everything. The 8 wants to own quality things and does what it takes to attain them. The 8 will work very hard for their income. You can be stubborn and you don't like to take advice. You exude a sense of well-being and prosperity, and people respect you on sight. Some will be threatened; a kind word will put them at ease.

The 9 Personality: The 9 Personality appears as a leader—the one we can count on to help us when things go terribly wrong. You have exceptional intuition and the insights you provide make others welcome your advice. In Numerology, the 9 is the most evolved number and you have the wisdom of an old soul. Spirituality is important to you and others perceive you as a good and trustworthy person.

Seven

The Power Name Number

What is the Power Name Number? When you add the Soul Number and the Personality Number and break it down to one digit, you will get your Power Name Number. This number represents the strength of your name and lets us know who you are.

Example:

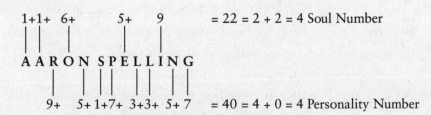

1+1+ 6+ 5+ 9   = 22 = 2 + 2 = 4 Soul Number

A A R O N S P E L L I N G

9+ 5+ 1+7+ 3+3+ 5+ 7   = 40 = 4 + 0 = 4 Personality Number

4 (Soul Number) + 4 (Personality Number) = 8 Power Name Number

Some of the most commanding people in Hollywood share the Power Name Number 8, which is the business-minded number. Aaron Spelling is considered one of the most influential television producers of all time. If you think about it, "show business" is all about making big money. There are a lot of very successful people with the Power Name Number 8, such as Madonna, Guy Ritchie, Antonio Banderas, David Duchovny, Elizabeth Taylor, Andre Agassi, Will Smith, and the list goes on.

▪ POWER NAME NUMBER DESCRIPTIONS ▪

The Power Name Number 1: When you have the Power Name Number 1, you have a strong desire to be the best. You set high standards for yourself and you expect excellence in all the people in life. As a result some people will feel under intense scrutiny and you need to let them know that you are coming from a positive place and that you really want to make their lives better. The Number 1 encourages you to strive for excellence. The Power Name Number 1 works hard and plays hard. As a result, you must find healthy ways to relieve your stress. Playing sports or working out at the gym are both ideal.

The Power Name Number 2: The Power Name Number 2 is the natural social worker. The Power Name Number 2 abhors conflict; if people are feuding, you want to resolve the situation. You are kind and really want peace. Having a loving relationship is very important to you. If there is discord, you're unhappy and the pain is easily read in your eyes. The 2s are usually the soul of tact, and are often found in the role of mediators. The 2 does not seek the throne, but does very well as the power behind one. Advice to the 2 is to choose very carefully those you work for, as you can be taken advantage of.

The Power Name Number 3: The Power Name Number 3 appears to be the consummate showman. The Power Name Number 3 is the natural communicator. You need to speak your mind, tell others what you think and how you feel. You should be in some area of performance, whether on the stage, in front of a classroom, or addressing a crowd in a lecture hall. Being onstage should be a natural for you—if not, it usually means scars from your childhood. The 3 is quick-witted and welcomes that round of applause!

The Power Name Number 4: The Power Name Number 4 is someone we look to as a solid base for us. You tend to be responsible, and your home is important to you. Sometimes you are too blunt and you annoy or hurt others unwittingly, so watch what you say. You have a strong need to acquire knowledge and you usually know what you're talking about. Just don't give too much unasked-for information about what can go wrong with a friend's pet project. You're probably absolutely right, but they might see it as negativity. Your loyalty and genius for organization are huge pluses and are very much appreciated in the long run.

The Power Name Number 5: This is a high-energy person. People can almost feel the electricity surrounding you. You can be an escape artist—it might be sex, drugs, alcohol, geography, or work. You are the celebrators of life; you want to travel, to see what's out there. You love to make things beautiful. You are the master party decorator—and parties can bring fascinating news, another favorite of yours, as you love a mystery and dig for facts. Stay busy, and within reason keep those frequent flyer miles going.

The Power Name Number 6: The Power Name Number 6 person is usually attractive in a way that goes beyond the physical. You present yourself well. There is magnetism to you. You want to be in charge, and your air of authority makes it easy for others to follow you. Damage control is your specialty and sometimes you get nervous when things go too smoothly. Relax, trouble is not necessarily around the corner. You are dependable to the point where you must seek a balance and learn to loosen up and enjoy the life you have so industriously built for yourself and your loved ones.

The Power Name Number 7: The Power Name Number 7 is someone no one completely knows, because you are often trying very hard to figure out just who you are, yourself. You are the keenest observer in Numerology, and 7 is the writer's number. When you share your observations, take care to choose your words, or you might offend the people in your life and not even know you've done it. There is gentleness to this number that I find when the Power Name Number 7 has come into a strong faith. There's a true spirituality to you that we can all benefit from.

The Power Name Number 8: The Power Name Number 8 is very strong, and you like to let others know exactly where you stand on any given situation. You collect things for sentimental reasons. You are drawn to quality and because of that you must find ways to generate a decent income. The Power Name Number 8 either makes lots of money or lets money slip right through their fingers; but money is an issue you must deal with in this lifetime. You need to be more open to other people's advice and know that the people in your life love you and want to help. You as a Power Name Number 8 do have to find ways to show the love that's in your heart, because you can be easily misinterpreted.

The Power Name Number 9: The Power Name Number 9 has a palpable energy. People see it when they meet you, and you have the ability to help others. The number 9 is the number of completion. You have tremendous intuition and insight about life, so much so in fact that you can intimidate others. For this reason you have to be careful not to say anything that might sound superior, however unintentionally. Let go of old family matters. The 9 can either live in resentment of their original family or feel too responsible for them. The 9 must embrace some sort of spirituality in order to attain true serenity. Take time to explore this dimension of your life. You have a lot of power, and it is to the 9s' credit that most of you use it wisely and are a real force for good in the world.

▪ POWER NAME NUMBER VS. DESTINY NUMBER ▪

Destiny is simply having the vision to realize your dreams and the perseverance to keep working towards them.

—C. PHILLIPS

The Power Name Number and the Destiny Number have the same placement in your name (this is the third number in the series of the five Primary
Numbers in your chart), but you can *only* get your Destiny Number from your
birth certificate name. You can always alter your Power Name Number by
changing the spelling of your name. *The Destiny Number can never be changed
because it is derived from the very first name you were ever given.* The characteristics of your Destiny Number will show themselves in your lifetime. It is important to note that if your Destiny Number and Life Path Number are a
Challenge Number to each other, it will take a little longer for your Destiny
Number to express itself. If you wish to speed up this process, you can change
or alter the spelling of the name you go by so that your current Power Name
Number is the same as your Destiny Number. Remember that while you cannot
change your birth certificate name, you can easily modify your current name to
help you accomplish your goals.

Take the case of singer John Denver. His birth name was Henry John
Deutschendorf (12/31/1943) and it added up to a 7.

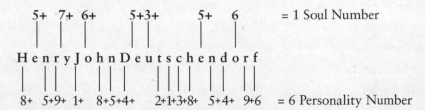

1 (Soul Number) + 6 (Personality Number) = 7 Destiny Number

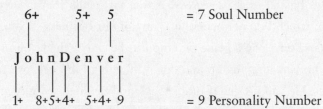

7 (Soul Number) + 9 (Personality Number) = 7 Power Name Number

What's interesting is that when he changed his name to John Denver, it became a 797. He took on the energy of the double 7 and the new name helped
speed up his birth number destiny, because of what the 7 represents.

First, the 7 is about having faith, but it's also about appreciating the natural beauty of this planet. I've never met a 7, even the ones who don't believe in God or question the process of God, who is not deeply affected by the beauty of the ocean, the mountains, the snow, the green grass, the flowers. When you listen to John Denver's lyrics, like "Rocky Mountain High" and "Sunshine on My Shoulder," he makes us feel his love for all of nature. When you hear that music, you feel the beautiful spirit that lives through his work

He also costarred in the *Oh, God!* movies. In the movie *Oh, God!*, in the person of George Burns, God comes down to earth to convince the world that He exists. This is Numerology typecasting! What better choice for that role of the doubting Thomas, who is later convinced, than John Denver, with all those 7s in his chart! You cannot look at a photograph of John without seeing his gentle spirit, and, of course, male 7s have great sensitivity because of that gentleness.

Before John changed his name, it would have taken more time to achieve his destiny, because his Life Path, which was a 6, is completely different from a 7. And in Numerology, 7 and 6 are actually Toxic—6 meaning family and home and the need to have children. He did have a child and that child loved him dearly.

His Attitude Number was also a 7, the air of mystery. John didn't want people knowing his business. As I said earlier, 7s do escape. Some through travel or work, some more destructively through food, alcohol, drugs, or sex. In John's case, he did it through alcohol. But we didn't know the extent of that until he died, which is typical of a 7's secrecy. It was the media that made us aware of his problem, which I do not believe was any of our business.

My sister met John Denver on a plane two months before he died. John sat with his daughter, who was jumping up and down, hugging him, her love for him bright in her eyes. He had his guitar on his back and radiated serenity and kindness. When my sister walked up and thanked him for the music he had given us, and the joy he had brought to her, tears welled up in his eyes. He was humble and grateful that somebody appreciated his gift. Here was a man who had such tremendous success, but he was still, at heart, a loner.

The Destiny Number gives you a glimpse of where you are headed as time goes on. The Life Path is the course you should take, but the Destiny Number represents a big part of your future and where you will end up. Although you may modify it somewhat by altering your birth name, the Destiny Number is always the power behind any change and will express itself throughout your life. The following are brief definitions of the Destiny Numbers.

The Destiny Number 1: Before you leave the planet, your destiny is to be number 1 at what you do. You are a leader, and need to be in charge. You push yourself the hardest and strive to be the very best at everything you attempt. When you have achieved one of your major goals, teach yourself to take time out and really enjoy the moment. With a Destiny Number 1, you will have all the time you need to realize your dreams. You must remember you are only human; it's okay to make mistakes on your way to achieving excellence. It would be wise to center your enormous energies—try yoga, or any of the other Eastern schools of meditation to achieve inner serenity.

The Destiny Number 2: Before you leave the planet, your destiny is to bring people together in peace and harmony. You are the consummate mediator; 2s make good judges, and are often active in civil rights work. Don't let your compassion overwhelm you. If you do not stay strong within yourself, you will not be effective in the work that means so much to you. You love unconditionally, and while you are a fine parent and mate, you will ultimately find a way to bring these qualities to the world at large. You have innate psychic abilities. Remember to not take on the pain of others, or you can be tempted to retreat within yourself. Your destiny is to stay in the world and create a better one.

The Destiny Number 3: Before you leave the planet, your destiny is to motivate and uplift other people. You are the communicator and can often be found as a motivational speaker, an actor, or a writer. On another level you could be striving to make people more beautiful as a hairdresser or designer of clothes or interiors. You always need to make things better and you succeed at this in a wonderful way. Be careful that in your need to counsel and heal you do not pick partners or friends who lead you into depression. Maintain your own equilibrium and balance. You are a joy to others; learn to control your emotions so you can also be a joy to yourself.

The Destiny Number 4: Before you leave the planet, your destiny is to leave something behind that we can all benefit from. When a 4 learns a skill, they become an expert, and because they want to share this knowledge, they make excellent teachers. This can be in teaching us how to do something better, or building something that remains after you are gone—a building, a collection, or even a beautiful garden. You are always instructing others, and you are a natural logician. A plus B must always equal C. You are the fixer, of everything from leaking faucets to faulty city planning. Be sure that you act upon your excellent ideas before worrying them to death in your head. Your instincts are sound; it is your destiny to act upon them.

The Destiny Number 5: Before you leave the planet, your destiny is to effect change. The 5 is the celebrator of life. You bring enchantment to the simplest things—5s are the party givers, the adventurers, and the innovators. The world needs the avant-garde and you are it. Your ideas may one day be standard, but you are always on the cutting edge. Be careful that your need for change does not disintegrate into escape through drugs or alcohol. A 5 is a natural detective and can detect what is not honest, or true, in a person or a government. An evolved 5 can help lead the world out of hypocrisy and into an honest exploration of life.

The Destiny Number 6: Before you leave the planet, your destiny is to provide a safe haven for yourself and your loved ones. Your "loved ones" usually expands to include all those who cross your path. You are the consummate parent and if you don't have biological children, you will parent your employees, your students, your pets, in short, the world. You have strong organizational skills, and the gift for making an environment beautiful, whether it's a homeless shelter or a halfway house. Anyone lucky enough to be under your care will feel loved and very safe.

The Destiny Number 7: Before you leave the planet, your destiny is to seek faith and the meaning of life. You are a spiritual being, and if you deny that aspect of your self, you will never find true peace. You need your solitude, but you also have a need to share your beliefs with others. You will often choose to do this through writing or music. Do your best to avoid becoming cynical from bad life experiences. You need to escape harsh reality, and you have to learn to do this in nondestructive ways. It's good for you to explore the world and to be near the ocean or a beautiful environment such as the mountains. Avoid drugs and alcohol. Meditation is a natural for you, and it will help you achieve the tranquility you seek.

The Destiny Number 8: Before you leave the planet, your destiny is to attain financial security. You must learn to understand the illusory nature of money. There are millionaires who are afraid to spend a dime; there are near paupers who share their little with others and feel like kings. You are here to learn that the universe will meet your needs. As an 8 you are drawn to quality and like to collect possessions that have meaning to you. The 8 may suffer hardships that can manifest in physical and mental pain. The key is for the 8 to keep their sense of humor and stay focused on their goals. If they do this, they will most certainly get what they really want out of life.

The Destiny Number 9: Before you leave the planet, your destiny is to achieve and lead others to a higher state of consciousness. To attain this, you must learn to forgive those who have hurt you in the past. You are strong and unflappable, and that is why people turn to you for leadership in a crisis. The downside of this is that you can sometimes seem unapproachable or even arrogant, but as we both know, you actually need and welcome love. Let people know when you need their help. *It is okay to ask for it.* As you grow, and learn to master a more balanced outlook on life, it is part of your destiny to teach others how to do the same.

Eight

The Birth Day Number

The Birth Day Number is the day you were born. It is the way you look, and how people will perceive you at first glance. Since the Life Path Number is who you really are, it is easiest when the Birth Day Number is either a Natural Match or Compatible vibration to your Life Path. However, if your Birth Day Number is a Challenge Number to your Life Path Number, you will always baffle the people who are in your life. If this is the case in your own chart, just be sure to let people know who you really are (your Life Path Number). It will help you to avoid unnecessary confusion throughout your lifetime.

▪ TWO CASE STUDIES: HARRISON FORD AND ALEC BALDWIN ▪

Harrison Ford is a bit of a mystery. He was born on a 4 Birth Day and is a 9 Life Path. These two Vibrations are a Challenge Number to each other. His Life Path 9 tells us why he is a successful actor and also a humanitarian. It is his 4

Birth Day that puzzles us. A 4 is not usually comfortable being in the limelight and answering questions. If you've ever seen Harrison Ford in an interview, you may have wondered, What is he really thinking? What's going through his mind? You can actually see that he is not quite in the moment. That would be an element of a 4 vibration, not a 9. So this would be an instance where "What you see is not what you get."

Alec Baldwin was born on a 3 Birth Day and is a 3 Life Path. This is a case of "What you see is what you get." Everybody knows that Alec is very open. Even when Kim Basinger broke up with him, he publicly expressed his broken heart to let us know how much pain he was in. He is now writing a book of essays covering this agonizing experience. The 3 Life Path often uses the written word to heal their emotional wounds. Politically, he said that if George Bush became president, he would leave the country. As we all know George Bush did win, and Alec is still here. He made that statement for dramatic effect—a typical thing for a 3 Birth Day to do, especially when they also have a 3 Life Path, which would encourage the same behavior. The 3 Birth Day Number is about communication and self-expression.

▪ BIRTH DAY DESCRIPTIONS ▪

The 1 Birth Day (People born on the 1st, 10th, 19th, or 28th): The 1 Birth Day appears as someone who is very cerebral, someone who takes pride in his or her individuality. You will appear to others as independent, creative, and very capable in a leadership position. The 1 Birth Day does their best work when they feel respected by the people they work for. If under too much scrutiny, the 1 Birth Day will rebel.

The 2 Birth Day (People born on the 2nd, 11th, 20th, or 29th): The 2 Birth Day appears as someone who can see both sides of every question. They are happy to follow, and work well in groups. The 2 Birth Day does not usually crave the spotlight, but they are inspirational to others. Those born on a 2 Birth Day are often psychically gifted, and don't be surprised when people ask you for that kind of advice.

The 3 Birth Day (People born on the 3rd, 12th, 21st, or 30th): The 3 Birth Day appears to be a joyous person and a faithful friend. While you appear to be artistic and imaginative, people will also see you as practical and, if a parent, a very good disciplinarian. The 3s are the great communicators, and people will often seek out your counsel. If the 3 Birth Day cannot find ways to be happy, they will become very moody. The good news is that they do bounce back quickly!

The 4 Birth Day (People born on the 4th, 13th, 22nd, or 31st): People will assume that the 4 Birth Day is orderly and good at detail. These are the managers of life and hard workers. People will look to the 4 Birth Day for those excellent qualities of loyalty and determination. If a 4 Birth Day thinks they are right about something, they will very seldom give up their position. To their credit, they usually have proof to back up why they feel the way they do. They must choose their words carefully and not be so blunt. The people born on a 4 Birth Day are often misunderstood. A kinder delivery is the key to better understanding from others.

The 5 Birth Day (People born on the 5th, 14th, or 23rd): The 5 Birth Day appears as a person who is quick-witted and fun, and people get a kick out of you! If there is an upcoming party of some kind, your presence can only make it better. People enjoy sharing their juiciest secrets with a 5 Birth Day. The 5 Birth Day can also appear restless, because the 5 gets bored easily. Finding ways to keep the mind stimulated (reading, art exhibits, museums, traveling, parties, etc.) is the key here.

The 6 Birth Day (People born on the 6th, 15th, or 24th): People born on a 6 Birth Day appear as a born nurturer, someone who craves love, friends, and companionship. When a 6 Birth Day walks into the room, you will feel their presence immediately. They have a dynamic energy. The world sees them as a solid personality, very responsible and capable of managing other people. A 6 Birth Day instinctively knows how to deal with children, and pets usually respond to them with instant affection.

The 7 Birth Day (People born on the 7th, 16th, or 25th): The 7 Birth Day is seen as one who must have some solitude on occasion. The 7 Birth Day is intellectual and looking for profound answers as to why we are here. Others may feel you are hard to know. People born on a 7 Birth Day often do not give themselves enough credit when they have accomplished something significant. They make a bigger difference than they realize. Music and nature have a profound effect on those born on a 7 Birth Day. They should have both in their day-to-day life.

The 8 Birth Day (People born on the 8th, 17th, or 26th): For those born on a Birth Day of 8, the world sees you as someone who desires quality of life. Most 8 Birth Days are willing to work hard. You like nice things, can be well organized, and would appear proud of the lovely family and home that you have acquired. People born on an 8 Birth Day can be accident-prone and must pay close attention to their health. Finding ways to stay healthy and safe should be a priority. People born on an 8 Birth Day are often accused of being unapproachable. The 8 Birth Day should make an effort to show their warmth.

The 9 Birth Day (People born on the 9th, 18th, or 27th): The 9 Birth Day is perceived as a people person. The world looks to you for advice—strangers ask you for directions. Everyone is quite sure the 9 Birth Day can help him or her. The 9 Birth Day exudes a confidence that makes people trust them completely, even with their innermost secrets. The 9 Birth Day can appear as being *condescending*, and must watch their delivery when communicating. The 9 Birth Day must establish healthy boundaries with their original family in order to stay happy and at peace.

▪ THE MASTER NUMBERS ▪

I get a lot of questions about Master Numbers from people who are born on the 11th or 22nd day of the month. Often they want to know why I don't talk more about Master Numbers, because somewhere along the way they've heard these are very special days to be born.

In some ways, they are right. The Master Numbers 11 and 22 do carry a particular power, which I will go into later. But first, let's see if you have a Master Number in your birth date. There are two places you can find the Master Number:

1) The day you were born is either the 11th or 22nd of the month.
2) When you are figuring out your Life Path Number, the digits of the month, date, and year add up to an 11 or 22 prior to the final breakdown.

An example of the second might be if your birthday were 1/3/1980. As you begin adding up the digits, you'll see that before you reach the Life Path you get a Master Number:

1/3/1980
$1 + 3 + 1 + 9 + 8 + 0 = 22$

If this were your birth date, you would have a Master Number in your chart. Two other examples are:

GEORGE CARLIN   CLINT EASTWOOD
Born 5/12/1938   *Born 5/31/1930*
$5 + 1 + 2 + 1 + 9 + 3 + 8 = 29$
$2 + 9 = 11$ $5 + 3 + 1 + 1 + 9 + 3 + 0 = 22$
The 11 is the Master Number.   *The 22 is the Master Number.*

What does it mean when you have a Master Number in your chart? It means quite simply that you should not kick back and relax in this lifetime. You have work to do. You have the power to make a difference, and your time on this earth can be used for a higher purpose. So, light a white candle, meditate, and ask the universe what it is you are here to do. Will you serve a greater purpose through teaching or writing thought-provoking books? Are you going to do it by designing wonderful buildings? Will you find a cure for a disease? The bottom line for the Master Numbers 11 and 22 is you often have a brilliant mind, and you need to put it to use.

▪ SOME WORDS OF CAUTION FOR THE MASTER NUMBERS ▪

Being a Master Number can be a blessing, but it can also attract indecisiveness and, in some cases, unhappiness. When someone feels a pressure to "master" their life, there can be a certain panic and insecurity. What if something goes wrong? What happens then is that all of your great ideas languish because you are afraid to act on them. The 11 and the 22 are prone to these fears. The Master Number 11 can study the Number 1 and know that some of the lessons will feel doubly true for you (because of the double 1 energy). The Master Number 22 can study the Number 2 and know that some of the qualities of that number will feel doubly true (because of the double 2 energy). The MOST IMPORTANT THING TO REMEMBER is that the Master Number ultimately still breaks down to a 2 and a 4 respectively. Embrace that final number and give yourself a break. What really falls on the Master Number is the question of finding out what it is you must do with your life. You will not be content until you do.

Being a Master Number does not make other people less than you. Whether you know it or not, your actions can sometimes make people think you hold yourself above them. Others may go on the defensive with you for no reason that you can figure. Be aware of this tendency and make an effort to put people at ease and be kind.

If you are Master Number 22, choose your words carefully, because you don't need to be blunt and verbally execute others, even though you are very gifted with words. It would be better to use your words in order to promote peace in your life and not conflict. As for the 11, you have that same problem, but for a different reason. When you have a double 1, that voice within tells you that you are not good enough, that you can never get it right. There is a defensiveness that comes from you and subconsciously you have your dukes up to protect yourself. Let them down, learn to meditate, learn to relax and work on ways to love yourself more, because if you can heal that fear within and still that negative voice, you will attract more joy and kindness into your life.

If your Life Path or Birth Day adds up to one of these numbers, please know that the only people given these numbers are the ones who are here to inspire others and serve humanity. Consider this a gift from the universe.

▪ THE POTENCY OF ZERO ▪

The ancients considered the 0 to be a gift of divine intuition, because it is without limit. Those who have a 0 in their Birth Day will have a clear, calm inner voice of spirituality. If you listen, it can change your life for the better.

If you were born on the 10th, 20th, or 30th, or if your birth date adds up to one of these numbers, before the final breakdown of one digit—whenever there is an 0, it can be a great blessing. There can also be a hidden 0 in your birth numbers the same way you might have a Master Number. Two examples are:

Jodie Foster
Born 11/19/1962
$1 + 1 + 1 + 9 + 1 + 9 + 6 + 2 = 30$

Debbie Reynolds
Born 4/1/1932
$4 + 1 + 1 + 9 + 3 + 2 = 20$

If you have a potent 0 you are one of those special people who can help others find their way. You have the ability to motivate, inspire, and uplift. Whether your number is a 10, 20, or 30 would determine how you would go about doing that.

The **10** would do it through mentoring, encouraging others to focus on achieving their dream.

The **20** would do it through love, by being completely supportive, encouraging others to go forward without getting in the way.

The **30** would do it through counseling, advising, in other words, communicating to help others get there.

The 0 intuitively understands the best in all numbers and the worst in all numbers. They have great empathy and make excellent problem-solvers. They are the caretakers, wanting to take care of others, but must be careful not to get battered and bruised to the point of having to shut down. You run the risk of being drained by anyone who is too negative.

When the 0 is in love, they want their significant other to feel so special that they will oftentimes downplay their own gifts so as not to upstage their partner. This is never a healthy thing to do. If the relationship ends, the people with the 0 energy will shut down and find it difficult to ever love again. The solution is to embrace their God-given gifts and share them with as many people as possible in their lifetime. It is important that they let no one stand in their way.

To quote Kahlil Gibran's *The Prophet,* "Never limp before the lame, deeming it kindness."

Nine

The Attitude Number

The greatest discovery of any generation is that a human being can alter his life by altering his attitude.

—WILLIAM JAMES

If you look at the Life Path Number of someone you're studying and it doesn't seem accurate, take a look at their Attitude Number. As you recall from chapter 2, the Attitude Number comes from adding the month and the day together and breaking that number down to one digit. Let's look at an example:

Julia Roberts was born on 10/28
$1 + 0 + 2 + 8 = 11$
$1 + 1 = 2$
Julia Roberts has a 2 Attitude.

While we know that the Life Path is the true sign of who a person is, the Attitude Number is what we *think* we are getting when we first talk to the person in question. The Attitude Number is what first impresses people. *If you have an Attitude Number that is a Challenge Number to your Life Path, then people don't know you.* They may think they have a grasp of who you are, but in truth they don't know what they're getting. As long as the Life Path and Attitude are a Natural Match or Compatible Number, then there is no problem.

One client called me because she was confused about the man she was seeing. He was born on August 6, 1961. She said he was very flirtatious and sweet at first, but as they started dating he was much more serious and very different from what she thought he was. I walked her through the numbers.

He was a 6 Birth Day with a 4 Life Path and a 5 Attitude. In this case, the 5 contradicted who he really was. The 4 is very serious and disciplined. Life Path 4s are inclined to work hard, but when they get home, they want to stay there and relax. Home is their haven. These characteristics can also be true for the 6.

The 5, on the other hand, is rarely at home. The 5 is always on the go, in search of excitement and variety. The 5 is the charmer, while the 4 is honest, dependable, and not out to charm anybody. In this instance, the girl was a double 5 in her birth numbers, so she was drawn to her beau's 5 Attitude Number. What she didn't realize was that all his other numbers were toxic to her.

Once we'd broken down his numbers, my client was able to stop feeling hurt and rejected when her man got quiet and contemplative. This is a great lesson to learn: Always check the Attitude Number to make sure it's compatible to the rest of a person's chart—as well as your own!

Let's take a look at our previous example, Julia Roberts. Julia has a 2 Attitude. The 2 is in love with love. This is the Attitude Number that can make you believe in romance. When Julia is on camera, we buy everything she's selling. When she's in pain, we hurt for her. Remember that scene from *Notting Hill*? She looks meaningfully at Hugh Grant and says: "I'm really just a girl, standing in front of a boy, asking him to love her." It brings us to tears—that's the 2 in action! But what is Julia Roberts' Life Path Number? She's a 7, which is someone who doesn't tell you everything they feel. So again, we believe we have a special connection with Julia because of her 2 Attitude, yet her 7 is shrouded in mystery and will not let us completely in. That's the difference between her Attitude Number 2 and Life Path Number 7. The 2 loves everybody, and the 7 is very selective.

▪ ATTITUDE NUMBER DESCRIPTIONS ▪

Attitude 1: This is someone who doesn't like to ask for help. They are completely self-motivated. They usually have issues with their self-esteem; they just don't think they're good enough. That's why they need praise from others. If you believe in them, then there's nothing they can't achieve; if you don't, they rebel.

Connie Chung	8/20/1946
Gloria Estefan	9/1/1957
Henry Ford	7/30/1863
Elton John	3/25/1947
Barbra Streisand	4/24/1942

Attitude 2: The 2 Attitude is easygoing. They tend to be the observer. They have a romantic streak and love is important to them. They're also intrigued with anything regarding psychic ability, and experience déjà vu. They have dreams that come true. They are in touch with their intuition and the metaphysical side of life. They do have compassion for people and are fascinated with people's stories. They are seldom bored.

Julia Roberts	10/28/1967
Harry Connick Jr.	9/11/1967
Mia Farrow	2/9/1945
Leeza Gibbons	3/26/1957
Janis Joplin	1/19/1943
Tennessee Williams	3/26/1911

Attitude 3: The 3 Attitude tends to be the joker. They have a sense of humor and are charismatic. The Peter Pan syndrome, they don't necessarily grow up. But when they're in a good mood, it's a big smile, bright eyes, and great conversation. If they're in a bad mood, you don't get to be happy around them. They have that effect on people.

Cuba Gooding Jr.	1/2/1968
Steven Spielberg	12/18/1947
Sarah Vaughan	3/27/1924
Truman Capote	9/30/1924
Clark Gable	2/1/1901
Alfred Hitchcock	8/13/1899

Attitude 4: The 4 Attitude is a list keeper. There are times when they become very quiet and you do not know what they're thinking. They're keeping track of all that's happening. You might find them surrounded by nature, or doing any form of repair, or construction. The 4 Attitude teaches all of us. They become an expert at their skill and teach us how to do it. They definitely will play devil's advocate; they make you see all sides. If they think you are being dishonest, they will confront you.

Woody Allen	12/1/1935
Bette Midler	12/1/1945
Vanessa Redgrave	1/30/1937
Sylvester Stallone	7/6/1946
Bruce Willis	3/19/1955

Attitude 5: The 5 Attitude is playful and fun. Here are examples of some clients. One of them sent me a picture of herself sitting on an elephant in Sri Lanka. Another for her fortieth birthday went down a raft in the Grand Canyon and on her fiftieth birthday was at the top of the Eiffel Tower. See how they need to go and explore this world? They can't wait to go and experience other parts of the planet, and if they get stuck in a monotonous situation, they can wind up playing the martyr. So, better for a 5 to get out there. It's all about adventure and excitement. They love to flirt, and they're usually the life of the party.

Roseanne Barr	11/3/1952
Goldie Hawn	11/21/1945
William Hurt	3/20/1950

| Ann-Margret | 4/28/1941 |
| Marlo Thomas | 11/21/1937 |

Attitude 6: The 6 Attitude is the nurturer. Male or female, they are taking care of everybody else. So if you have a child with a 6 Attitude, they act as if they are your mother or father. They're the ones in charge; they don't want you telling them what to do or how to be. They feel the most useful when things are out of control and they are fixing it. If it's peaceful, they don't know what to do with themselves. They definitely take care of other people and they're usually great with children or running a business. When a 6 enters the room, we are drawn to them like a moth to the flame.

Gracie Allen	7/26/1902
Warren Beatty	3/30/1937
Johnny Carson	10/23/1925
Jamie Lee Curtis	11/22/1958
Michelle Pfeiffer	4/29/1958
Frank Sinatra	12/12/1915

Attitude 7: With the 7 Attitude you don't get to know what they're thinking or feeling. They keep to themselves and are introspective. They must continue studying the quest of why they are here: The 7 Attitude has no problem asking direct questions but will look at you suspiciously if you ask them even one. They will reveal themselves slowly as they go. They can shut down and make you feel they are not remotely interested in what you are saying, but the joke is on you because they are the ultimate observers. They don't miss a thing.

Lauren Bacall	9/16/1924
Alec Baldwin	4/3/1958
Shirley Jones	3/31/1934
Sean Penn	8/17/1960
Kathleen Turner	6/19/1954

Attitude 8: The 8 Attitude has no problem telling you what they really think. They can be a little too blunt, so it is best to keep their sense of humor and focus on the positive things in life. More often than not, when I see an 8 Attitude, they are reading investors' magazines or brainstorming on how to improve their lives, and establish financial security. If they have family, then they want to be a good provider. The flip side of the 8 Attitude is that money can seem completely unattainable. Money will slip right through their fingers. The 8 Attitude must treat each day as a chance for a new beginning. They have to let go of the past, or they will harbor negative thoughts that will interfere with today's potential happiness.

Nicolas Cage	1/7/1964
Peter Sellers	9/8/1925
Suzanne Somers	10/16/1946
Gene Wilder	6/11/1935
Shelley Winters	8/18/1922

Attitude 9: The 9 is the leader. At work they'll not just do their job but everyone else's. Wherever a 9 goes, people will look to them as the person in charge. Their way of life is basically "Show me what to do, and I will do it." If they have any emotional scars from their childhood, they need to let them go. If they do not, it can lead to depression. They are very quick to help others, but they must learn to establish healthy boundaries so as not to be drained emotionally.

Jim Carrey	1/17/1962
Hillary Rodham Clinton	10/26/1947
Greta Garbo	9/18/1905
Rita Hayworth	10/17/1918
Ricardo Montalban	11/25/1920
Sonny Bono	2/16/1935

Ten

Repeating Numbers

When a particular number repeats itself in your chart, and it is not the same as your Life Path Number, it will also have a profound influence on your life. Although you must fulfill your Life Path in order to be happy, a repeating number in your chart cannot be ignored. Of course, if the repeating numbers in your chart do include your Life Path Number, the traits of your Life Path Number will be intensified.

We'll take a look at the charts of Christopher Reeve and Angelina Jolie to study the effect a repeating number can have. Then we'll examine Elizabeth Taylor's chart to show the impact of a repeating number when it is the same as the Life Path Number.

Christopher Reeve
8657**6**, Attitude 7

Breaking down Christopher Reeve's birth numbers (9/25/1952), we see that his Life Path Number is a 6. My first thought is that that's the father number, the kind of person who absolutely feels they need to have children. So it's no surprise that he had two children from a previous relationship and another one with his current wife. This is a man who wouldn't have felt complete if he did not have kids.

You know the 6 Life Path is good at solving problems; that's when they're at their best. When life is calm, they think, What? It's too good to be true. The 6 is magnetic, and when they come on the scene, we say, "Wow, who's that?" And let's face it—it took serious magnetism to play one of the greatest superheroes of all time! This guy was dynamic and America fell in love with him.

His Birth Day Number is a 7, and you 7s have an inborn sensitivity. This may have been why for so long people falsely accused Reeve of being gay. We all heard the rumors, even before he kissed Michael Caine in *Deathtrap*! People had that feeling about him, even though it wasn't true. But that's the 7 . . . they're very gentle people.

Reeve has an 8 vibration in his soul, and when you have an 8 in your soul, it means you suffer. You learn the hard way. You don't take advice well, and unusual things do happen to you. Life isn't necessarily smooth sailing.

He also has a 5, which is in the power of his name. The 5 likes excitement, travel, and adventure, and is ambitious. Reeve was a very active man who did all kinds of sports; as we all know, he was taking part in an equestrian competition when he had his accident.

The repeating number 7 in his Birth Day means that he's someone who needs to have faith. Clearly his very foundation has been tested in this lifetime. If you've listened to any of his interviews since the accident, you can hear that he believes recovery is possible and is doing everything he can to help the doctors learn more about spinal cord injuries. Recently he has regained some feeling and movement in his fingers, and has begun to speak again without his respirator. That's the 7's conviction; they believe there's nothing you can't do.

Angelina Jolie
96645, Attitude 1

Angelina Jolie was born June 4, 1975. This means that while she was born
on a 4 Birth Day, she is a 5 Life Path. When I look at those numbers, I know
that she has the kind of duality in her chart that leads to confusion. The 4 Birth
Day in her chart longs for security, a home, and a family, but her 5 Life Path
wants the free will to do whatever she wants. Angelina needs to explore the
world, and do things that are unusual and different.

Angelina and Billy Bob Thornton met on a movie set, and without much
forethought, impetuously married. Billy Bob was also born on a 4 Birth Day,
and is a 5 Life Path. Because of the 4 Birth Day, 5 Life Path conflict in each
chart there were, in effect, four people in the relationship.

By all reports, they were incredibly kinky, and sex was their priority. They
also carried small vials of each other's blood around their necks. They bought
tombstones and funeral plots for themselves, and the whole love affair seemed
macabre.

When I examined her entire chart, I knew that Angelina was destined to
change, because her name numbers were 9, 6, 6. A 6 is the mother number and
she had a repeating number 6, which told me the traits of the 6 would ultimately shine through. The 9 denotes the humanitarian. Well, as time went on
Angelina did indeed begin to deal with those parts of her personality.

Eventually, Angelina went to Cambodia and when she saw the death, de-
struction, and starving children, she felt called upon to help. She also found the
little baby boy she later adopted and named Maddox. When Angelina and Billy
Bob first got together, I had said on a talk show that if reality should ever catch
up with them, the relationship would be over, and that's exactly what happened. When she brought Maddox back to the United States, within eleven
days of Angelina and Maddox's homecoming, the marriage was over.

Angelina, however, with a 6 in her soul, is completely fulfilled as a mother.
Angelina also has a 9 in her chart, which is the number that deals with old family scars, and so at the same time as the adoption, she ended her relationship
with her father. She didn't want to continue to deal with the unresolved an-

guish she had from her childhood. She felt that he had done as much damage in her life as she was willing to take and she had to let him go.

Little Maddox has become her world. She has stated over and over that she hasn't been romantically involved with anyone in over a year and a half, and although she misses that part of her life, she doesn't want to take a chance on a destructive relationship harming her child. She's even stopped drinking, because of her fear that if she ever drank too much and he needed her in the middle of the night, she wouldn't be mentally clear for the child.

Angelina was chosen to be an ambassador for the UN, which validates her compassionate side, shown in her Soul Number 9. She is making a tremendous difference by speaking out on behalf of these poor children in Cambodia and is very much making the world a better place. As a Numerologist, I am not surprised; she is after all doing it "by the numbers." But, as a person, I am truly impressed with the way she has transformed her life.

> ## Elizabeth Taylor
> # 98898, Attitude 9

Elizabeth Taylor is an 8 Life Path. As I've said, 8s go through a lot in this lifetime. If you look at her history, this woman has always had physical problems and has always overcome them. She has battled her weight as well, but just like the 8 she is, she's quite a fighter and has always come back the winner.

Elizabeth Taylor is not only an 8, she's a *triple* 8! When a number comes up several times and it is also your Life Path Number, the characteristics of that number are magnified. In this case, all of those 8s in her chart explain her love of collecting flawless diamonds. That's the perfect hobby for an 8 to have. When I say an 8 is about mastering money, I mean that if someone with this number had to choose one of three items, he or she will invariably pick the most expensive, just because it looks the best. They're really into quality—something Elizabeth Taylor exudes.

Her Birth Day Number, 9, makes her the natural leader. If a 9 does something good, we follow; if the 9 does something bad, we follow then too! Good or bad, the 9s are our leaders; this is very true about Elizabeth. For most of her life her face on the cover of a magazine would sell more copies than any other subject, because people were always fascinated by what she was doing. Not because she was always on the screen doing movies, but simply because we couldn't get enough of her. I believe a good part of this is the dynamic power of her numbers.

The 8 and 9 are toxic to each other in numerology, so with a chart like hers (98898) you can be sure she has lots of inner turmoil. To some, she appears cold and aloof. Even though she wants to be close, it can be difficult.

In looking at the Numerology of some of the men she's been with, I found that three of her loves were 2 Life Paths, meaning they were vulnerable people. She's drawn to this type—think about her friend Michael Jackson. Other sensitive men she was close with include Roddy McDowell, Montgomery Clift, and James Dean. What draws her to them and them to her is her 2 Attitude. They feel very connected to her because of this shared Vibration.

▪ REPEATING NUMBER DESCRIPTIONS ▪

Here are the numbers 1 through 9, and what each number means when it repeats itself in your Numerology chart:

Repeating Number 1: It means you must strive to be the best at everything you do. You must overcome the little voice in your head that repeats "Not good enough."

Repeating Number 2: It means you need to love and be loved in order to be happy. You must overcome being too sensitive. It is okay not to feel everybody's pain.

Repeating Number 3: It means you must find ways to communicate, whether it is through speaking or writing. Do what it takes to keep your wonderful sense of humor, and always believe in magic.

Repeating Number 4: It means you must find ways to continue learning, and stop letting great ideas live and die in your head. Take a chance! Just do it! You will be pleasantly surprised.

Repeating Number 5: It means you must find ways to celebrate your life, and never let someone else control you. Go out and explore the world. Experience all that is new and exciting. Establish balance to avoid falling into a depression.

Repeating Number 6: It means you must nurture and take care of the people in your life, starting with yourself. Overcome your pride and let people know when you need help. It is okay to let down your guard.

Repeating Number 7: It means you must have your time alone with nature in order to find your true spiritual self where there is no hypocrisy. You must overcome your constant need to escape and find healthier outlets such as keeping a journal, going on a cruise, or perhaps exploring the Seven Wonders of the World.

Repeating Number 8: It means you must occasionally allow others to help you instead of always doing it yourself. You have the ability to be a great success or a great failure. There is no gray area for you. Life is a state of mind. Put out positive energy and it will come back to you.

Repeating Number 9: It means you must let go of all the old pain from your childhood. Share your responsibilities instead of taking on the whole burden yourself. No one can read your mind. Let others know what your needs are so that they can give back to you.

Eleven

The Intensity Number

When you break down a name, every letter has a number, so whatever number comes up the most is considered an Intensity Number because it is intensely inside you.

To show how this works we'll use the name Bette Midler.

Three 5's

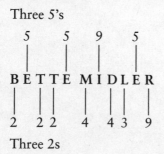

Three 2s

Bette Midler has three 5s and three 2s. She's got the 5, which means she's passionate, adventurous, she gets bored easily, and can get herself in dramatic situations. If there's a fear, it is that of monotony.

The 2 is sensitive and aware and really in touch with their feelings. It's two totally different energies in one person. It means she has command of her feelings, and if you think of her performances, that's clear. When she sings a song, she owns you. She owns the room but she has a real kinship with other people. Even though the 5 wants freedom, the 2 needs people. It makes for never a dull moment around her.

Look at the Intensity Numbers as someone's hidden agenda. If you see someone's birth certificate, you see the day they're born, you see their name, and it's interesting, but if you feel there's something missing, you'll find it in the Intensity Number. It could be that final ingredient.

Intensity Number 1: This means you have a tremendous awareness of self, you're strong-willed, you do what it takes to be the best at what you do, you can lead and you never stop. It's a constant movement forward. What does it mean? I want to win, I like to win, I'm going to win. If I see several 1s in a person's name, I know they're competitive, no matter what their Life Path Number.

Intensity Number 2: Again, with the 2 Intensity, it's the warm place that they seek. The 2s don't like to be alone, so it's the need for love. If you have a lot of 2s in your name, chances are, if you are single and working, you are not happy. You need that partnership. It is also a very psychic energy with amazing gut instincts.

Intensity Number 3: The joker, celebrator of life; creativity is a big part of your life, you mix well, you're social; 3s have an enjoyment of people, a playful quality. An intensity that means they never grow up; there's always a childlike quality in their eyes at any age. A 3 Intensity should be in any field where verbal communication is a prerequisite.

Intensity Number 4: The 4 is the seeker of truth, and is all about teaching. They are opinionated and feel the need to express their opinion. They are the one to look for in terms of doing it right, but must be careful not to let all those great ideas die in their head. They have to put them into action.

Intensity Number 5: My automatic reaction as a Numerologist to a 5 Intensity is: "You like sex." Every single time they laugh and say, "You bet I do." It's romantic and fun . . . the candles, the lingerie, the beauty. This Intensity says, "How can we make this a special event, not just typical?" The 5 Intensity is someone who wants to party and enjoy themselves and if they're not careful, they get themselves into trouble. For the 5 Intensity, life is all about passion.

Intensity Number 6: The 6 is the nurturer, so if it's a man, he's rescuing the damsel in distress and if it's a woman, she has a mate who's her little boy. Intensity 6s need to realize they don't have to do it all. They are magnetic, and you will be drawn to the 6. They don't know how to share responsibilities. They feel they have to do it all or it won't get done. So show them you can be there for them.

Intensity Number 7: Always an air of mystery. They don't want you to know their business. You cannot pry. If there are many 7s, there is a great spirit there. They are here to find their faith, and if you hold someone with a lot of 7s, you are going to feel that gentle, sweet spirit. When angered, they can make biting remarks that sting. The 7s do keep thoughts to themselves, so don't take their silence personally.

Intensity Number 8: The 8 is a number for success. It is business-minded. They're going to do what it takes to succeed in this lifetime. They tend to be the workaholic. The key is financial success. That's the intensity of the number 8. They have to learn to pay more attention to the people in their lives, for whom they work so hard in the first place. The 8 Intensity needs to learn to take advice to avoid being victimized.

Intensity Number 9: The 9 is charitable and cares deeply for people. They have a strong sense of wanting to go places. They should travel, look at the world, keep a journal, write their thoughts down and let go of old pain from their past. When they need assistance, they need to ask for it. The 9 Intensity should not resist leadership positions. They are very good at being in charge.

Twelve

Finding Your Perfect Mate

When you're looking at a relationship and want to know how compatible you are, the two numbers that you should pay close attention to are the Life Path Number and the Attitude Number. Ideally, your Life Path Numbers and Attitude Numbers will either be a Natural Match or a Compatible Number to each other. If they are a Challenge Number, then you will have some difficulties. The third important factor is the quantity of Numbers you and your partner have in common. If you have three or more of the Primary Numbers in common, then it is considered a Soul Mate Connection. What a Soul Mate Connection really means is that whether the relationship is good or bad, when it ends, it is never really over. It can be someone who teaches you *exactly what you do not want* in your life ever again, or makes each day feel magnificent just because the two of you are together.

Note: Be sure to break down the numbers of the *name you call* your love interest when you do your personal numbers. For example, if your partner's name is Robert Smith, but you call him Bob, use Bob Smith when you break down the name. If your name is Cynthia Thompson and he calls you Cindy, then break down the name Cindy Thompson when you compare your numbers.

▪ WHAT TO LOOK FOR IN A PERFECT MATE ▪

What is a Natural Match?

Natural Match Numbers are the numbers that are truly alike. They come in sets of three. The first set is 1, 5, and 7. They are the mind numbers. The second set is 2, 4, and 8. They are the business-minded numbers. The third and final set are 3, 6, and 9, which are the creative-minded numbers. When a Natural Match meets, it is an automatic connection. The relationship tends to flow. There is an immediate understanding. You do not have to explain to a Natural Match why you do what you do, because chances are they would do it the exact same way.

What is a Compatible Number?

These are the numbers in Numerology that you can get along with, but you may have to explain your actions to each other from time to time. A Compatible Number will enjoy your company, and be willing to work things out if the relationship gets off track.

What is a Neutral Number?

A Neutral Number is a vibration you will feel indifferent about at first. As the relationship develops, it can go either way—peaceful or an all-out war. You need to experience the Neutral Number on a case-by-case basis before drawing any conclusions. It's important to note that not every vibration will have neutral numbers.

What is a Challenge Number?

Challenge Numbers are the numbers that really do not understand you. It is as if you speak two different languages. Hurt feelings and misunderstandings are very common when two people come together who have Challenge Numbers in their chart. It is nobody's fault. It is just different vibrations flowing in different directions. Note: Some Numerologists insist on calling the Challenge Number a "Toxic Number." I refer to this number both ways throughout the book. So "Challenge Number" and "Toxic Number" are interchangeable.

▪ EVERY NUMBER CONNECTION CHART ▪

Here is a list of all 9 numbers and what their connection is to each number. This applies to *any* number when you are comparing your charts so that you can see which numbers are a Natural Match, Compatible, Neutral, or a Challenge Number to each other. That would include when you compare your: Soul Number, Personality Number, Power Name Number, Birth Day Number, Life Path Number, Attitude Number, and your Destiny Number.

1 VIBRATION:
    Natural Match Numbers: 1, 5, and 7
    Compatible Numbers: 2, 3, and 9
    Challenge Numbers: 4 and 6
    Neutral Numbers: 8

2 VIBRATION:
    Natural Match Numbers: 2, 4, and 8
    Compatible Numbers: 1, 3, 6, and 9
    Challenge Numbers: 5 and 7

3 VIBRATION:
    Natural Match Numbers: 3, 6, and 9
    Compatible Numbers: 1, 2, and 5
    Challenge Numbers: 4, 7, and 8

4 VIBRATION:

Natural Match Numbers: 2, 4, and 8

Compatible Numbers: 6 and 7

Challenge Numbers: 1, 3, 5, and 9

5 VIBRATION:

Natural Match Numbers: 1, 5, and 7

Compatible Numbers: 3 and 9

Challenge Numbers: 2, 4, and 6

Neutral Numbers: 8

6 VIBRATION:

Natural Match Numbers: 3, 6, and 9

Compatible Numbers: 2, 4, and 8

Challenge Numbers: 1, 5, and 7

7 VIBRATION:

Natural Match Numbers: 1, 5, and 7

Compatible Numbers: 4

Challenge Numbers: 2, 3, 6, 8, and 9

8 VIBRATION:

Natural Match Numbers: 2, 4, and 8

Compatible Numbers: 6

Challenge Numbers: 3, 7, and 9

Neutral Numbers: 1 and 5

9 VIBRATION:

Natural Match Numbers: 3, 6, and 9

Compatible Numbers: 1, 2, and 5

Challenge Numbers: 4, 7, and 8

▪ A POWERFUL COUPLE: BILL AND HILLARY CLINTON ▪

Bill Clinton   Hillary Clinton
8/19/1946   10/26/1947
68512, 9 Attitude   55183, 9 Attitude

Let's look at how they are connected. They have three numbers out of five, which helps explain why the partnership works and why it has not ended in spite of their very public marital strain.

Their Attitude Numbers are identical (9). Their Life Path Numbers are Compatible (2 and 3). They have three numbers out of five in common (1, 5, and 8), which makes them Soul Mates. They have every ingredient I look for in a promising long-term relationship.

Since a Soul Mate Connection can be good or bad, the first question you should ask yourself when you study your charts is, "Even though we have a Soul Mate Connection, am I happy in this relationship?" I say that, overall, Bill and Hillary are. I think there is tremendous fulfillment because their missions are similar, even though they have separate agendas. With their Attitude Number 9, each is a leader and people want to watch them.

The number 8 is the politician number and the number for making money. All 8s learn the hard way. Bill and Hillary have gone through Whitewater, Monica Lewinsky, the impeachment and many other controversies. But in joining forces, they have overcome all of their major difficulties. Bill Clinton served two terms in the White House, and Hillary went on to win the Senate seat for the state of New York by a landslide.

The 1 is independent. So this is not about being lovey dovey. It is about winning; and no one can dispute how good they are at that. The 5 can get into dramatic situations involving passion, which we had to suffer through over and over again in the newspaper headlines regarding Bill. Sometimes the 5 winds up playing the martyr, which Hillary (a double 5) could do—as the wronged wife—but she chooses not to.

Hillary's Life Path Number 3 is here to motivate and uplift people, and his Life Path Number 2 is to promote peace and harmony. Do you remember the joke, who would Hillary Clinton's husband be if she hadn't married Bill? The answer: the president. Because with her 3 Life Path, and the determination that governs her, nothing would have stopped her from becoming first lady. She's the push. She's so powerful in her own way that she pushed him forward. Because 2s follow, they don't always lead. In this case, he is a 1 Birth Day and a 2 Life Path. That means yes he's independent and motivated but sometimes likes to kick back. She never stops. The quotation "Behind every great man is a great woman" sums up this partnership.

What we're really looking for is the answer to what makes some couples work out together and others not. In numbers, Bill and Hillary were meant to be together. They have an understanding, whether we comprehend their relationship or not. We can sit in judgment of their relationship, but it is working for them.

A LOOK AT BILL AND HILLARY'S ACTUAL CHART

EXPLANATION OF NUMBERS	BILL'S	HILLARY'S	COMBINED
SOUL NUMBER What you feel inside. Not necessarily what people see.	6	5	Challenge
PERSONALITY NUMBER A face you show the world.	8	5	Neutral
POWER NAME NUMBER This Number represents the strength of your name. It is the most important number in your name.	5	1	Natural Match
BIRTH DAY The way you appear to people.	1	8	Neutral

EXPLANATION OF NUMBERS	BILL'S	HILLARY'S	COMBINED
LIFE PATH The number that you need to fulfill in order to be happy. The most important number in your personal Numerology.	2	3	Compatible
ATTITUDE NUMBER The first impression people have when talking to you.	9	9	Natural Match

How to Analyze Your Charts: Take a look at your charts. *If you find you have one or two Challenge Numbers*, just know you will have a couple of bumps in your road together, but nothing you should not be able to overcome. *If you have three Challenge Numbers*, it means you will always have to work at the relationship to keep it healthy. *If you have four or more Challenge Numbers and one of them is your Life Path Number*, you need to ask yourself, what are you really getting out of this relationship? Do some soul-searching, and if you still feel it is worth it, honest communication and major compromise are what it will take to keep this relationship. Remember, Neutral Numbers are to be judged on a case-by-case basis.

▪ KNOWING YOUR PREFERENCES ▪

The key to finding your perfect mate is to know what you're looking for. Moreover, knowing yourself well enough to know what works best for you and the kind of person who will complement your life.

Whom you meet is whom you're well enough to meet. When you go through a hard time and start to heal, there are certain people who fall away because they can't be in your life anymore. It's all about your personal journey. For instance, 2 vibrations, when I meet them, are healthy and nice people. Technically it's a Life Path I get along with.

Yet I have friends who can't stand 2 vibrations because they think they're over-emotional, or too needy. Look at your own patterns to decide whom you cannot be with—and you will see it clearly when you start breaking down the numbers of the people in your life and start to see your history. Certain numbers will come up again and again. When I see the same numbers in one person that I've already had trouble with in another person, I don't put myself through it again.

Pick vibrations that are easier for you to get along with. That's what's fun, making it a numbers game, realizing that no one's really out to get you.

Example: A 1 Vibration. Let's say I'm a 1 Life Path and I meet a fellow 1 Life Path, and every time I meet a 1, they're backed up with me. They are competing with me, and seem to think I feel superior to them. No matter what I say, it turns into a competition. Even though I'm compatible to a 1, perhaps it's best that I not be with a 1. We're always going to be in a struggle with each other, wondering who's going to win. Better to pick a number that's less competitive. Since the 2 Vibration does not like to compete, the 2 could be a good choice.

There is a positive and negative side to every number. You will learn through this book how to do a personal reading for yourself. You should write down the relationship you are in today. If you are not in a relationship, check out the one from your past that you never got over. Then go back to see if there is a pattern there. Next do your mom or your dad, whoever you feel had a bigger impact. Then do both, whether it was a great relationship or a bad one, just to see what those numbers were.

Let's say as a woman, you got along beautifully with your dad. Well, if you met a guy with your father's numbers, there's a good chance you'd be compatible with him. Unfortunately, what we often do, subconsciously, is pick the numbers of the parent we didn't get along with so we can now "fix" that relationship. Of course we all know that we can't change the past. Once you see the pattern in numbers, you can make a new choice.

▪ YOUNG AND IN LOVE: GWYNETH AND CHRIS ▪

Gwyneth Paltrow   Chris Martin
Born 9/28/1972   Born 3/2/1977
18912, Attitude 1   15622, Attitude 5

EXPLANATION OF NUMBERS	GWYNETH'S	CHRIS'S	COMBINED
SOUL NUMBER What you feel inside. Not necessarily what people see.	1	1	Natural Match
PERSONALITY NUMBER A face you show the world.	8	5	Neutral
POWER NAME NUMBER This number represents the strength of your name. It is the most important number in your name.	9	6	Natural Match
BIRTH DAY The way you appear to people.	1	2	Compatible
LIFE PATH The number that you need to fulfill in order to be happy. The most important number in your personal Numerology.	2	2	Natural Match
ATTITUDE NUMBER The first impression people have when talking to you.	1	5	Natural Match

When Gwyneth Paltrow and Chris Martin first started dating, I was asked to give my opinion on the relationship—whether or not I thought that it was a good one. I was very impressed with what I saw in the numbers. The most important number that Gwyneth and Chris have in common is their Life Path Number, and that very fortunate number for them is the number 2. The person with the number 2 is someone who seeks love, peace, and harmony. It's the number that I always say makes for a great partnership, as a 2 will value his mate and respect the other's feelings. A 2 couple would enjoy a lovely home, and a visitor would notice a fresh scent in the air. There will more often than not be candles burning and music playing.

It is the 2's nature to be very open with affection. There was a touching picture of our couple in *People* magazine when Gwyneth left the doctor's office newly pregnant with her first child. Her happy husband knelt beside her and kissed her stomach. Absolutely what a 2 would do, and what another 2 would appreciate. The 2 couple is so eager to please that hardly can one partner get out a compliment before the other responds in kind. Like the cartoon birds Heckle and Jeckle, it becomes almost comical:

"After you."

"No, after *you*."

"Oh, you're so nice."

"No, *you're* so nice."

"Oh, I love you."

"No, no, *I* love *you*."

In addition to the Life Path 2, Gwyneth and Chris share the same Soul Number 1. When you have the same Soul Number with your partner, it means that what fulfills you in your heart is the same for both. The 1 number is the number of ambition, so both will be striving to be the best that they can be in their chosen professions.

Here we have two ambitious people in the entertainment business. Chris Martin is a singer/performer and Gwyneth Paltrow is an actress, so they are not in competition with each other. While the baby is a highlight for both of them, it is especially important for Gwyneth. She needs to feel she has a family. Gwyneth has a 9 in her chart, which gives her issues with abandonment. She adored her father, and while she knows he did not leave her willingly, she can't help but feel abandoned. She's trying to feel whole again, and the starting of a new family will give her that cycle of completion and beginning again.

Chris Martin has the number 6 in his chart, and 6 is the father number. His chart tells me he will be a wonderful father, very loving and kind. Also, he's got the need to rescue the damsel in distress. Gwyneth was in tremendous pain when her father died. It was Chris who was the one who comforted her and made her feel loved. Not only is he a 2 Life Path, but he was also born on a 2 Birth Day. This means that with Chris, what you see is what you get. He doesn't play games and he knows who he is.

Gwyneth has a double 1 in her chart, and she often questions herself. Amazing as it may seem to the world that is in awe of this fine actress, she often doesn't feel "good enough." Chris would be the man to dispel her insecurities. Overall, they are very lucky they found each other and should be wonderful parents to an equally lucky child.

▪ AFFIRMING YOUR PERFECT MATE ▪

The basic affirmation to attract a fulfilling love:

"I welcome a loving, nurturing relationship with a man (or woman) who will be emotionally available to me: who will be honest, passionate, and funny, who will be my equal and will be my life partner."

How many of you have just read the above affirmation and thought, Oh, I wish I could have that kind of relationship. If you are single, you have the opportunity to create a love that is rewarding for yourself, perhaps for the first time in your life. I feel we all put on a pair of faulty mental glasses when we are searching for love. Our "mental glasses" can only attract what we believe to be true. So if you have never had a great and loving relationship, how do you attract one?

The only way is to reprogram the subconscious mind. This is done by repeating certain words over and over again, until your subconscious believes it. With a new belief system, you will become a magnet for someone who is loving, emotionally available, someone who's nurturing and your equal.

Now I know for a fact this works. I've had many clients—well over 500 different people—attract a wholesome partner and many of them have gotten married. What do you have to lose? It is certainly worth repeating these words over and over again, fifteen to twenty minutes a day. Remember, you are reprogramming your mind, so you must do this affirmation every day. YOU WILL GET RESULTS!

I am also living proof. Right now I have by far the greatest love relationship I have ever known, and it was definitely done by using the above affirmation. This man is truly the personification of being "honest, passionate, funny, and my equal." Needless to say, I am thrilled!!

One of my clients said, "Glynis, all of the men I meet cheat on me." What's her belief? Men cheat on her. So men *do* cheat on her. I suggested she add to the affirmation the words: "... **and who will be loyal to me.**"

On that note, ask yourself what your issues are, because whatever they are, they have to be negated in your love affirmation.

A male client complained that the women he meets have no sense of humor, so he wrote in, "... **someone with a sense of humor.**" Perhaps you'll add, "... **someone who is honest,**" if that's your issue. If you are affirming it, you will attract it. Can't find a man who will commit to a relationship? You say, "... **who will love commitment,**" and the next guy you meet will probably say, "Hi, I'm Sam and I love commitment." It happens so fast, you'll laugh.

In the case of a pattern of dating passive/aggressive men, perhaps a woman might add something like, "... **who is strong in a sincere way.**" The next man would then be nurturing, loving, and supportive.

A recurring lack or problem in your life comes from negative feedback in your subconscious. You've been playing those inner tapes for quite a while now, so begin today to turn your life around with positive affirmations. *There is enough good in the universe for all of us.*

The following chart tells of a profound love story that is sure to inspire you. It is a story that makes one realize extraordinary love is possible.

▪ TRUE LOVE BY THE NUMBERS: MARION AND DAVID ▪

Marion Cooper
Born: 11/5/1911
61751, Attitude 7

David Kaufman
Born: 5/14/1914
62857, Attitude 1

EXPLANATION OF NUMBERS	MARION'S	DAVID'S	COMBINED
SOUL NUMBER What you feel inside. Not necessarily what people see.	6	6	Natural Match
PERSONALITY NUMBER The face you show the world.	1	2	Compatible
POWER NAME NUMBER This number represents the strength of your name. It is the most important number in your name.	7	8	Challenge
BIRTH DAY The way you appear to people.	5	5	Natural Match
LIFE PATH The number that you need to fulfill in order to be happy. The most important number in your personal Numerology.	1	7	Natural Match
ATTITUDE NUMBER The first impression people have when talking to you.	7	1	Natural Match

All my life, I bore witness to the great love affair between my grandmother Marion Cooper and my step-grandpa, David Kaufman. They were together for fifty-seven years, and when Dave passed away, Marion followed within six weeks. Their story is a testament to the power of numbers.

Before she met David, Marion was married to Jackson Parks. Jackson was my biological grandfather, and I adored him, but he was Toxic to Marion in Numerology. Jackson was born on a 6 Birth Day and a 6 Life Path, Marion on a 5 Birth Day and a 1 Life Path. A 5-1 cannot be controlled by anyone, and the 6 Life Path has to be in charge, or at least feel that way. This meant their most important numbers seriously challenged each other. Well, not surprisingly, after my mother was born, they wound up divorcing. Marion became a single mother and began working full-time.

Six years later, she met David Kaufman. My grandmother had by then become a magazine writer who interviewed celebrities for a living. She wrote for *Photoplay, Movie Life,* and other leading fan magazines of the day. David was a young newspaperman—later becoming the first television critic for *Hollywood Variety*—but this was 1943 and there was no TV as yet. They met at a press party, and sat down and talked for hours. (Note: When two people have the same Birth Day Number, in this case a 5 day, there is an instant rapport.) When looking at all of their numbers, they shared the numbers 5, 6, 7, and 1. Remember, when you have 3 numbers out of the 5 Primary Numbers in common, you are Soul Mates. By the end of the evening David asked my grandmother to marry him. Now what makes this even more extraordinary is that David was thirty-two years old, had never met a woman he would even consider asking to marry, and yet instinctively knew he was meant to be with Marion.

Why? David was born on a 5 Birth Day, with a 7 Life Path, and a 1 Attitude. Marion was born on a 5 Birth Day, had a 1 Life Path, and a 7 Attitude. Their birth numbers were completely Naturally Matched, and when this happens, it is truly heaven on earth. David began to pursue Marion in earnest, asking her daily, "Will you marry me?" A week later they were married in Vegas and really did live "happily ever after." For all the years they were married, David sent Marion a red rose every Tuesday to commemorate the day they had met.

The love between them was extraordinary, and even as a child I could feel their loving connection. Both were writers and journalists, so they had that world to share, and they also loved films and travel. The 1-5-7s need freedom to come and go—and their need to come and go was so well synchronized that they never spent a night apart. They also shared a 6 Soul Number, which is the nurturing number, and when they gave birth to my aunt Laurie, it made their souls feel complete.

When Marion was eighty, a brain aneurysm that had been lying in wait her whole life ruptured. Delicate brain surgery was performed, and while she was unconscious she had a near-death experience. Marion later told me that she'd had the often-reported sense of crawling toward a light through a tunnel. She remembered thinking, You've always wondered what it would be like to die, and it's not so bad, is it? As she continued, she saw a shadow in the tunnel, and thought, Oh, I hope that's David! When she turned and saw that it was, she yelled, "David!!" So strong was her joy at seeing him that she felt herself pulled back into life. Then she awoke.

My grandmother lived another ten years—and they were tough ones. She broke two bones and eventually ended up in a wheelchair, but she had David by her side the whole time. After ten years of caring for her, David's own health began to fail, and a few short months later, he passed away. Just two weeks after his death, Marion went into a coma and within weeks, she had joined him.

I believe Marion made a karmic agreement in the tunnel during her near-death experience to stay on this planet as long as David lived. Every day through that last decade they were together, David took the tenderest care of her. He loved her with all his heart, never once complaining about his lack of freedom to travel or socialize. And Marion never complained of her increasing disabilities. They both knew their extraordinary love was a gift, and that it was an honor to be in each other's lives. Theirs was the kind of love that we all deserve—a love we can consciously bring our way through the thoughtful use of Numerology.

▪ WHAT IF YOUR NUMBERS ARE NOT COMPATIBLE? ▪

As you are learning, the Life Path Numbers are the most important numbers to look at when you're judging romantic compatibility. But what if you're already in love with someone whose Life Path is Toxic to yours? Does that mean you should get out right now?

Numerology is a science of numbers, *but it's also a science of hope*. Once you learn the meaning behind the numbers, you'll start to see a whole new dimension to your relationship—meaning you can figure out ways to keep it healthy before it turns bad. I'm an optimist—as long as we live in the positive of our numbers, there really is no such thing as a truly Toxic number. They are a Challenge, for sure, but you can overcome them. Here's a story:

I have a 3 Life Path client, Katie, who was having difficulty with a coworker. Everything he said she misinterpreted, and she continually felt he was attacking and ridiculing her. When she broke down his numbers and did his chart, it turned out all five Primary Numbers were Toxic to her in Numerology. This made her laugh! Suddenly she understood why they were always having disagreements. She was then able to stop blaming him and actually befriended him, because she understood where he was coming from.

If you're a Challenge to me, I'm a Challenge to you. In the same way, if you're a Natural Match to me, I'm a Natural Match to you; we can just lift an eyebrow and the other understands. This is so freeing; neither party is "bad"— we're just predestined to see life differently. Numerology helps us learn to have more consideration for each other.

When you do a Numerology breakdown of family—your mother, your husband, your ex-husband—and you think about the people you never got along with, you'll begin to see a pattern. Perhaps all of their charts contain a 5 or a 6, both of which are incompatible with you. Or maybe your charts say you *should* be compatible, but clearly in this lifetime, you are not. I want everyone to realize how very individual your charts are; you can get the numbers easily enough, but in order to see what's going on with your individual story, you need to do some homework with the people in your life. No two people are exactly the same, even if their numbers are.

If you tell someone what their numbers reveal, and they fight you on it, there's a really good chance that they don't want you to know what their strengths and weaknesses are. They don't appreciate that you read them like an open book. Use Numerology as your own trump card. You don't always have to share the information with the person you are dissecting.

As a Numerologist, I have seen many happy couples who are technically considered "Toxic" to each other. You can make your union work no matter what your numbers are. If you have understanding, there can be true unity and peace.

It is important to understand that any substance abuse can ruin even the most favorable numerical combinations. If you are in a situation like that, I strongly recommend one of the Twelve-Step Programs. Alcoholics Anonymous is the original program, and now there is help for everything from drug use to sex addiction. You can find your local chapters in the white pages of your telephone directory.

Below are the Relationship descriptions of how each Life Path Number gets along with each Life Path Number.

1–1: Let's talk about the 1–1 relationship. When these two join forces, they are dynamite, because both are competitive and both want to be number one. In harmony, they can run a business and turn it into an empire. But the minute they compete with each other, the minute that jealousy or conflict rears its ugly head, they are in desperate trouble. Harmful competition makes them volatile, angry, and vindictive. So, to two 1s, I say, "Look straight ahead. Look at the vision of what you are creating together." Since they are critical of themselves inside, 1s will manifest their criticism outside. Let's say they want to take over a company. If they work together, their criticism works to an advantage, but if they get into the habit of putting each other down, they can quickly become very small, very petty. The relationship goes from "We can do anything" to "We can do nothing. We can't even get out of this house, we're so busy fighting." My advice is to stay on track, and to not lose your real focus.

1–2: A 1–2 relationship can be very good. Let's say a 1 Vibration is running a business and in charge of what they do there, but the 2 partner, who always needs hugs and kisses, reminds them to love, and to continue the romance which brought them together in the first place. See how that can be a balance? They can have the best of both worlds. The 2 gets the benefit of the 1 making a living and the 2 makes their home lovely, warm, and ready for whatever life brings. The way the 1–2 relationship can go wrong is if the 1 is always working and constantly on the go. As a result the 2 feels abandoned and starts reaching out for more attention, making the 1 feel trapped. I've observed these numbers enough to know that while the 1–2s are different, their partnership can work if each respects the other's needs.

1–3: This combination can work because the 3 is usually very good at praising and acknowledging the partner—something the 1 definitely needs. The 1 is ambitious and can help the 3 to focus and achieve their dreams. Their conversations are stimulating as is their physical relationship. The 1–3 couples often keep the romance alive by role-playing in the bedroom. No one enjoys assuming a role more than the 3 and nobody enjoys a new conquest more than a 1. The thing for this couple to avoid is being too critical of one another, as neither vibration handles criticism well. The 3 can become depressed, and the 1 may seek out another who will make them feel special. These two must learn to choose their words carefully. That said, if they do team up, they do extremely well together.

1–4: These vibrations tend to do better in business than in love. In love the 1 is spontaneous and has high energy, while the 4 can feel uneasy in any situation that is out of their control. The 4 needs time to think things through and make a plan. The 1 will have trouble waiting, and the 4 will be appalled by the 1's impatience. In business, however, there is an understanding that if the 4 has a good idea, the 1 can put it into action immediately. In this situation, the 4 will appreciate the follow-through of the 1, because 4s are known for having great ideas that never come to fruition. This is a case where the couple must be able to accept each other's differences and compromise. Two very different energies here, but love can conquer all.

1–5: The 1s and 5s are both mind numbers, with an ability to understand each other and their need for freedom and independence within the relationship. There can be tremendous compatibility for the 1–5 couple. The 5s need to avoid unnecessary drama—taking on everyone else's problems, for example—because the 1s will lose respect and become acidly sarcastic. In the most successful 1–5 couples I have seen, both partners work and are "almost too busy for each other." They don't see each other as much as they would like, and when they get together, it's a celebration! There is such excitement in just getting to share the stories of their adventures. Oddly, too much togetherness can destroy their strong bond.

1–6: These two can have a power struggle with each other. The 6s need to feel that they are in charge, and taking care of everything and everybody. At the same time the 1 has a strong desire to be, as the number suggests, first. These two powerful egos will clash, and the end results can be devastating. On the other hand, if they have a joint venture in which each plays an important, but separate, role and each feels valued and is acknowledged for it, this match can work out just fine. The phrase the 1–6 must avoid is, "If I don't do it myself, it will never get done." These words must never be spoken in this relationship. Give each other praise and encouragement because, as you know in your hearts, there is nothing you cannot achieve.

1–7: Because 1s and 7s are both mind numbers, the 1–7 couple never stops thinking and processing. The danger here is that they will dissect their partners until there is nothing left. There are some real differences here. The 7s, at times, need to be left alone to reflect and regroup. The 1 can take this personally, and I caution the 1 not to do this, just wait for the 7 to come back and things will be better than ever. If the 1 continually finds fault with the 7, things will get worse and will destroy what could have been a great relationship. The 7 has insights that are very valuable to the 1, and the 1 (as in the 1–4 relationship) is a great motivator, able to turn the 7's dreams into practical reality.

1–8: The 8s can do well with a 1 because the 1 is ambitious and wants to make money. If they join forces in business, they are dazzling. In love, it's extreme: It's either excellent or it's a disaster. These numbers do not handle criticism well. I believe it is because their own personal standards are so high, they always feel they are somehow not measuring up. They have this loud inner voice putting them down, and the last thing they need is their significant other giving negative feedback. That's why if a 1 does fall in love with an 8, it can start out great and the next thing you know, they can't stand the sight of each other. It is imperative for the 1 to acknowledge all the good that the 8 brings into their life. Sometimes, the 8 needs to let the 1 win in the relationship. It can be as simple as letting the 1 win a disagreement you are having. The words "You were right, honey, what was I thinking?" can go a long way when trying to make the 1 feel loved and appreciated. Compromise is the key here and then a solid partnership can develop.

1–9: This can be an exciting relationship because, in Numerology, 1 is the beginning number and 9 is the completion number. This means that all the energy contained in the numbers between 1 and 9 can be experienced in the relationship, which can truly be fascinating. The thing for the 1 to avoid is thinking the 9 is being superior. The 1 can get defensive and angry and the 9 will have trouble tolerating it. A problem for the 9 is learning to let go of the past, while the 1 is very much in the moment, and is aggravated by the rehashing of old issues. If this couple can learn to live in the present and fully embrace what they have, they will thank the heavens every day, simply because they have found each other.

2–2: Above all else, the 2 Vibration needs love, lots and lots of it. There is no greater love than a 2 with a 2, because they both have the same need to give and receive love, and they're going to have great respect for each other. The 2s will always be very polite to each other, always making sure the other is taken care of. What can go wrong? Well, if one of them feels under attack they can lash out in such a way as to deeply wound their partner. When the smoke clears, the angry one is filled with remorse, while the other often cannot let it go. I strongly advise the 2 to avoid going to that ugly place, because in Numerology, their love is truly a gift.

2–3: The 2–3 combination can work very well together. The 3 is the communicator and entertainer, and the 2 makes an amazing audience. The 2s can be very supportive and don't tend to crave the spotlight, so this can be a great combination when it comes to love. There will be a lot of laughter and great physical chemistry. If a 3 energy hooks up with a more competitive number, there is friction, whereas the 2 has no problem being behind the scenes as long as they are appreciated. The 2 is comfortable in that position, and it's the only number in Numerology that is sincerely like that. If a 2 is reading this and says, "Wait, I like to be number one," I say, check your other Primary Numbers. Chances are you'll find a 1, or some other competitive number there.

2–4: The 2–4 combination can be extremely fulfilling. The 2s need to feel loved and 4s likes to provide security, so when it comes to home and family, this can be the perfect match. The 4s are builders and like to have a plan, and 2s are peacemakers. When both numbers are living in the positive energy of their vibrations, it makes for one of the better combinations that I have observed in Numerology. The problem the 2–4 can have is that 2s like to know where they stand in a relationship at all times, and when a 4 is troubled, they retreat within. If the 2 pushes for communication, the 4 will withdraw even more. I caution the 2 not to take the 4's silence personally. This is the time for the 2 to focus on other things in their life that they may be neglecting. When the 4 feels they have solved the problem inwardly, they will come back to the 2, confident and ready to show their love and appreciation for their patience and understanding.

2–5: The 2–5 combination will definitely take some work. The 2s need their families and their homes. The 5s need the freedom to go out and do whatever they feel is important. They also need to feel they are in control of the couple's activities. If the 2 feels unloved or neglected, and expresses this to the 5, the 5 may feel they are being smothered. The 5 needs to take time out to acknowledge the 2's kindness and love, so the 2 will not panic and feel the relationship is in trouble. If either one believes his or her way of living is the only way, the relationship will not last. The 5 will provide excitement and the 2 will provide a warm, safe environment in which love flourishes. The 2–5 must celebrate their differences and realize that with each other they can have a richer experience of life.

2–6: The 2–6 is a great pair for love. The 6 represents family and 2 represents love. By bringing these two energies together as a couple, the association can last a lifetime. It is important that the 2 praise and acknowledge all the good the

6 does for them. The 6 must let the 2 know how much they appreciate all the little things the 2 does to make their life romantic and sweet. The 6 tends to be very direct and must learn to choose their words with care, so as not to hurt the 2's feelings. The 2s are easygoing until they feel defensive; then they become the terrible 2s. If this happens often enough, the relationship, no matter how strong, can turn sour. An awareness of each other's true needs is the key to this relationship's success.

2–7: It is very important for the 2–7 couple to be living in the positive side of their numbers. For example, if a 7 has not found faith and is still cynical, the 2 will become drained trying to make the 7 happy. In Numerology, the 2 and the 7 are considered naturally psychic, and when they are in tune with this gift they are a joyous couple. However, 2s like to communicate verbally with their partners at all times, and 7s sometimes have nothing to say. There is a dialogue playing constantly in the 7's mind, which can make the 2 feel very lonely. The 2s have to find something of their own to focus on—whether it's taking a night class to learn a new skill, or doing volunteer work with the old, or the sick, to utilize their loving nature. This is a good couple for working together in the healing professions. With patience and the right kind of work, these two can be blissfully happy.

2–8: The 2–8 partnership can be very effective in business. If they are a couple in love, they should look at their relationship as a business, with one number taking care of the family, and the other providing the financial security needed to run the household. If the 8 is the breadwinner, he must be careful not to treat the 2 like a possession, but as a person he values greatly. The 8 must try to be aware of the 2's feelings, because 8 is a very direct number and can easily say things that cause the 2 pain. The 2s are usually comfortable following a leader they like, and 8s need someone to follow them. Things can go wrong when a negative 8 feels victimized and blames everyone for what is not going right in their life. This is hard on the 2, who so wants to please and make others happy. The 2 will tolerate a great deal, and then suddenly they cannot go on. If you are in a 2–8 relationship make sure the 2 feels treasured and the 2 will see to it that the 8 feels loved. With understanding, this combination can win at love.

2–9: The reason this one works is that the 2 Vibration needs love and is very open about letting you know how they feel, and when in a relationship with a 2, the 9 is reminded that someone gives a darn about them. Remember, 9s are usually the ones who are leading the pack. When they do something good, we want to follow; when they do something bad, we'll still follow them. Up there at the head of the pack, if they're overwhelmed, does anyone have a clue? Everyone thinks that the 9s are just fine, they always seem to be in control. Well, the 2 will intuitively realize that something is wrong. The 2 is a caretaker and will say, "Are you okay?" They'll also take that time out to say, "I'm so impressed with what you did." What can go wrong? The 2s hate to be alone, and when 9s are out there saving the planet, they must remember to come home and shower love on the 2 who needs them most. If they do not, it can cause a rift in an otherwise loving relationship.

3–3: The first thing I would say is if the 3–3 is living in the positive side of their vibration, then any measure of success is possible. If both 3s are succeeding in a creative way and are financially stable, this can be an incredible relationship. If, however, they meet at the beginning of their careers and are struggling, it is easy for them to escape into each other's arms and be irresponsible. Running away from problems becomes the norm and when the bills are due, they come as a serious wakeup call. If both are in a creative field, such as acting, watch for trouble when competing with each other. The minute one becomes critical of the other it can lead to verbal warfare. The 3s believe in magic, and if they choose to empower each other, they can achieve whatever they desire.

3–4: The 3–4 duo can be a tricky one: The 3 is spontaneous and likes to take chances, whereas the 4 likes to map everything out and have some kind of plan before making a move. The average 4 likes to know all he can of his future. The 3, on the other hand, believes in seizing the day. The 3 and the 4 are going to have to make a real effort to make their partnership last. It will take compromise on both sides. For instance, the 4 will make a statement, consider it sound, and figure that's the end of the conversation. Wrong! The 3 is the natural communicator and will always have an opinion. And the more the 3 talks, the quieter the 4 gets, behavior which will drive the 3 crazy. If you are in a 3–4 combination, here's what you do: the 4s need to embrace the 3s' passion and love of life—they tend to be lucky, so the 4s should not be afraid to let go a little. The 3s need to be grateful for the 4s' loyalty and the solid base for living that they provide. They can fly a little higher knowing that a strong net is there to catch them should they fall.

3–5: The 3–5 couple will delight in each other's company. They will be the life of any party. Since the 5 is the natural detective, and the 3 likes to hear every story (they have to be in the know), these two fascinate each other endlessly. Needless to say, these energies do very well in the more creative professions. Money can be a problem if they do not pay close attention to the budget and the bills. If possible, they should get someone else to manage the money. I always say that 3s and 5s are like bright lights and, as bright lights, they can attract bugs. As a couple, they have to be careful not to take on too many people and projects that take all their energy; otherwise, they can become so drained that they have nothing left to give each other.

3–6: This can be a terrific partnership because these two are of like minds (creative). The 3 will enjoy the magnetism of the 6 and will encourage them to be strong. The 6 will make the 3 feel taken care of and loved. I have also seen this combination of numbers do very well in business. An important consideration is what the 3 does for work. Whether it is show business or hairdressing, if the 3 feels like a star in life, no effort will be too much for him to see that the 6 is happy and feels secure. If the 3 or 6 does not feel appreciated, it can destroy an otherwise perfect match. Sexual chemistry is one thing they will not have to worry about. It's always there. This couple needs to take time out for romantic interludes, and remember that the best escape is in each other's arms.

3–7: This is a case where opposites attract. The number one thing a 3–7 couple have is phenomenal physical chemistry. While the 7s are elusive and will not always be willing to share their thoughts, the 3s love to say what they are thinking and feeling at all times. The 7 will admire the charismatic personality of the 3, and can learn to appreciate people by seeing them through the loving eyes of the 3. The 3 will embrace the words and wisdom of the 7 when they feel like expressing themselves. The 3s have a love of people, where 7s can only take so much human contact before they have to excuse themselves to be alone—preferably with nature. If the 3 can accept this part of the 7, all is well. However, if the 3 feels the 7 is not listening to them and begins to question the 7, the 7 will shut down even more. Then the 3 will feel unloved and rejected, which can lead to depression. If the 7s are in turmoil, they can be cynical, which can rob the 3 of their natural vitality. If these two numbers are living in spirituality, they will enrich each other's lives greatly.

3–8: This relationship takes a bit of work. The 8s can be caught up in their goals to the exclusion of all else, making the 3 feel neglected, as though they are not a priority. The key to success here is for the 3 to respect that the 8 is trying to provide security, and the 3s also need fill their own cups with interesting activities. Then when the 8 and 3 get together, they do not dwell on their separations, but share their adventures and treasure their private moments. If the 3–8 go into business, especially if the 3 somehow stars in the enterprise, the partnership is often enhanced. An 8 living in the positive side of the vibration is very good with money, and sees that the partner is provided with the finest things. What to avoid: If the 8 feels victimized and blames others, the 3 will get fed up and want to move on. This does not have to happen and 3–8s can have a very loving and financially stable union.

3–9: This can be a relationship filled with laughter and great conversation. It is imperative that the 9 not let their old family issues interfere with their present relationship with the 3. The 3 will take the 9's problems to heart, and when they cannot help solve the problem, the 3 will eventually give up in despair. This relationship is based on verbal communication. The 3–9 relationship is intense and can lead to huge arguments with passionate reunions in the bedroom. This couple must make time for romantic getaways. The 3–9s enjoy new people, places, new ideas, and will have opinions on everything. The 3–9s agree with each other most of the time, but as in all relationships, a spiritual base is what will keep this union healthy.

4–4: Two 4 Life Paths can do well with each other because they both have a need to feel secure—they need to know the bills are paid. They respect each other. They go out of their way to make sure the other feels his or her needs are being met. He, as a 4, might take care of her by being the handyman or computer expert, and she, by taking on the job of homeschooling their children (remember, the 4 is the natural teacher). The 4–4 relationship is usually long term because 4s don't like to date, and once they make a commitment, they want it to be forever. So they tend to do well in love. They also excel in business, because they share the work equally, and are good with the details—both of them taking notes and making sure everything is handled in the company.

4–5: The 5s are high-energy people. They like to create excitement around them. How the 5 would communicate is not how the 4 would communicate, which sometimes causes misinterpretation and hurt feelings. There can be stepping on toes without meaning to. The 4s are very direct whereas 5s would be more charming, even going out of their way to make a person feel comfortable. A 4 will stay in a relationship that is not healthy just because they don't like change. A 5 might feel trapped and want to get out. Truly respecting and listening to each other is the key to this relationship.

4–6: This combination can be great in a marriage, especially when children are involved, as the home and the need for security fulfill both vibrations. If it is the female who is the 6, the old saying, "If Mama ain't happy, ain't nobody happy" applies here. If the male is the 6, he needs to feel he is king of his castle, and the 4s understand this. What to avoid: The 4s are notoriously blunt and they need to choose their words carefully in order to avoid a true battle with the 6 partner. This is the kind of union where children make the parents want to keep the family together at any cost. If there are no children, then it could be a business or home they have invested in that they do not want to lose. In any case, they will make a monumental effort to stay together.

4–7: These two often get together for security, and that's what keeps them a couple. Passionate love is often lacking, and I have found that 4s and 7s sometimes step outside the marriage for a love affair and yet never leave their partner. Now, if you're in such a relationship don't put this book down and punch your partner in the nose; most 4s and 7s are absolutely and perfectly faithful.

Take steps now to find out what your partner needs from you. One real plus in this relationship is that the 4s providing security makes it possible for the 7s to bring their brilliant ideas to fruition. What the 7 brings to the 4 is fascinating insights on almost everything. The 4s tend to be homebodies, and the 7s can encourage them to look at the natural wonders of the world. The 4 will have life experiences they never would have without the 7 as their guide.

4–8: The 4–8 combination can work because both are business minded, and their goals in life are similar. The 4 can map out a plan so that the 8's big dream can be achieved. Since the 4 and 8 learn the hard way, they will have to really focus to make their dreams come true. Their life lessons are often difficult, but the payoff is well worth it. Perseverance is the key word in this partnership. The 4s need to avoid dropping verbal bombs that cause instant arguments, and 8s need to avoid blaming others when something goes wrong. The 8 needs to remember that when you blame someone else, you lose all of your power. Both vibrations tend to be hard workers. As a couple it is imperative that they remember to stop and smell the roses. To verbally express love can be difficult for both, especially if they are hanging onto past resentments. This is something the 4–8 will need to work on, especially if they decide to have children. These people are fiercely loyal and protective of their loved ones. Investing money early in this relationship is a wise decision, and they can start building that nest egg they need to feel safe. When the 4–8s put their minds together, the sky is truly the limit!

4–9: The first thought I have is that the 4s and 9s handle their lives completely differently. The 9 likes to help the world in a big way, such as public speaking at charity events, working the phones at a crisis center, etc. They give so much that they sometimes feel no one is giving back. The 4 must be sympathetic to the 9's humanitarian instincts. They should lend an ear when the 9 can no longer take the stress. The 4 will be impressed with the knowledge and insight the 9 possesses; having an intelligent partner means a great deal to the 4 vibration. The 9 must realize that home is the 4's sacred space where they can rest and plan their future. The 4s are not as social as the 9s. The 9 must accept this and know that the true gift the 4 offers is their complete loyalty to the relationship. The 4 must try not to be too critical of the 9's family—the 9 will take it to heart and it could lead to the deterioration of the relationship. If the 4 and 9 concentrate on each other's strengths, the relationship will flourish.

5–5: The phrase to describe this relationship is "Never a dull moment." Two 5s are like racing cars going 150 miles an hour—with no one having bothered to check the brakes. Will they crash or won't they? Only they know. Friends will all have opinions on this relationship, but it is best that the 5s discuss any real problems with each other. There will always be some kind of drama coming their way. The 5s should try not to get too involved in other people's problems. Sexually, the chemistry is usually wild and explosive. The 5s are not very good at or interested in their money, though they like to spend it. If possible, they should have a business manager take care of it for them. Travel is important to keeping this love affair going strong. Ideal jobs for this double 5 couple would be pilot and stewardess, or a detective and his partner. The 5s are also natural entertainers. The way for this to last is if the 5s both love their work and if their lives are action-packed. If they are not, their lives can degenerate into a soap opera. Stay on top of your 5 energy! No one can celebrate life like a 5, let alone two 5s.

5–6: Although technically considered Toxic, the 5–6 combination has surprised me many times. The 5s are the ones who like freedom and the 6s are the ones who like their home. Here's a look at two clients of mine who made it work: The husband is in the entertainment business and is a double 5 in his birth numbers. He's constantly traveling, and they have children. His Attitude Number is a 6, which is the father energy. So when he comes home, he likes the role of being Daddy. The 6 started a coffee shop—one of those drive-through stands—and now she and her friend own three of them. That business keeps her cup full (no pun intended), and she's doing well. Instead of lamenting that her husband's always gone, she's doing so much with her own energy that she's excited about her own life as well. The 6 is above all a nurturer, and she sees the kids benefiting because both parents are successful role models and these children know whatever they set out to do they can do, because look at Mom and Dad. If she were living on the negative side of the 6, she would lament, "Where is he? He's not home for dinner, he's not here to look at my beautiful home, and all the cleaning I've done." By having a business and children, she doesn't go there. It's come up enough for me to notice that these numbers can work even though in Numerology the first thought would be "no."

5–7: It is imperative that a 5–7 couple travel and enjoy the world together. If they stay in one place too long the 5 will become restless, and because the 7 is psychically in tune with their partner, it will make the 7 uncomfortable. The 5s need constant movement, whereas the 7s need only to slip into their mind and that is where their adventure is. The 5 must adjust to the 7's need to be alone. In truth, both need their private space. When 5s give 7s an embrace, they can feel their gentle spirit. Although a 7 is difficult to figure out, the 7 can see right through their partner, so there is no point in making up a story. The 5s are natural detectives, so they actually have a good chance at cracking the mystery of the 7. Either way, it keeps the relationship interesting, and it can be very exciting in the bedroom. When you do find a place to settle down, make sure it is near a body of water. The water has a profound effect on the 7. The 5s also appreciate nature's beauty. I caution the 5 not to push the 7 into a verbal confrontation. They will not respond until they are put on the defensive, then they will counterattack and verbally execute the 5, from which the 5 will have difficulty recovering.

5–8: The 5–8 combination works because they're both dynamic personalities. The 8s are often accused of being workaholics. They're so busy trying to achieve their goal, they don't stop to smell the roses. If you put a 5–8 together, they have a blast. They both enjoy the luxuries of life: fine wine, elegant hotels, the best cuisine, beautiful jewelry, soft fabrics, etc. If a 5 comes up with a grandiose idea, like owning a restaurant that provides good food and entertainment, the 8 would get all the paperwork together to turn it into a huge financial success. Well, on the business level, they're going to work effectively together, and on the personal level they're going to enjoy each other. If the 8 is working and making money, the 5 can play even more. They're both doing what they love, and they don't get in each other's way. What can go wrong? The 5 can have a wandering eye, and the 8 will not tolerate it! Some 8s are frugal and want to keep all the money in the bank. The 5s will not put up with that. A 5 is here to celebrate life in a big way, the 8 better just give in and join them. If they do not, it can be the fatal blow to an otherwise wonderful union.

5–9 This is a case where empowering each other to achieve greatness is extremely important to both of you. The 5–9s love being winners in their own life, but also like spending time with people who have attained their own personal goals. The 9s set out to conquer the world and the 5s turn on the charm to help make it possible. If they do have children, the 5–9s will be good parents. The 5 will make sure there are plenty of days for the children to feel special (making holidays and parties magical is one of their gifts). The 9 will teach the children how to make the world a better place through practical means like collecting signatures for local issues, gathering clothes for the homeless, and so on. But the 5–9 can get so busy that they may lose sight of each other. Taking breaks from their separate lives to be together will keep this union going strong. Jealousy has no place here; it can ruin a 5–9 relationship faster than any other emotion.

6–6: Marriage, home, and family may as well have been invented for the 6. The average 6 would not be complete without something to parent, be it a family or a corporate empire. They want to take care of everybody. What a dynamic couple! Since they are the natural interior decorator, you can imagine that their home is going to be beautiful, and filled with wonderful furniture, artifacts, and food. There is a doubting streak in the 6; they must be careful to not be nervous when things are going smoothly. "It's just too good to be true" is an expression practically invented by the 6. It is imperative that they not repeat this, because 6s are powerful people and they can indeed think themselves into misfortune. They have to be able to accept the love they have found, and say, "Yeah, we found each other and we deserve this love."

6–7: This union will take some work, but it does have possibilities. If the 6 and 7 are living in the positive side of their numbers, then the 7 will be spiritual and the 6 will provide a lovely home where they can be together. The 7 needs space but will welcome the 6's company so long as the 6 does not disturb the 7's concentration. They cannot interrupt this time of meditation that the 7s need to feel at peace. When the 6 is troubled, the 7 must pay close attention, and not tune out what the 6 is communicating. If they do, the 6 will be deeply hurt, and have a hard time forgiving the 7. The 6 and 7 pride themselves on being good parents and will play an active role in their child's life. If any substance abuse is involved, then it is a whole different story. It is wise for them to live near a lake, river, or ocean because of the calming effect water has on the 7. The 6 needs a home they can turn into a safe little haven. The 7 should encourage the 6 to use their creative energies and start their own business. If the 6 and 7 have the same spiritual base, this relationship can last a lifetime.

6–8: This can be a very good match. The 8s are business minded and the 6s are magnetic. When this impressive duo strides into view, everyone will notice. The 8s usually have big ideas and the 6 helps to turn them into reality. The 6s also make sure they have a comfortable home to relax in. The chemistry is always there, but because they are so busy, they have to be spontaneous enough to make it happen, anywhere, anytime. The physical contact will give them that burst of energy they didn't even realize they needed. The 8s pride themselves on pleasing the 6s in the bedroom and the 6 should not be hesitant in telling the 8 what is needed. They should be careful not to expect them to guess—speak up! Tell the 8 what you like. They are not mind readers. The 8 must try to avoid feeling victimized and blaming other people when things go wrong. The 6 will try to make everything better, but will soon lose patience if the 8 does not snap out of it. Otherwise, the 6 will encourage the strength of the 8, and the 8 will be proud of the 6 partner they have been blessed to share their life with.

6–9: The 6s and 9s are excellent in business and personal relationships because they intuitively know how to give and take with each other on all levels. They respect each other, and thoroughly enjoy being together. It's hard to impress a 6 Life Path. They're easily jaded, but 9 is the highest number, and they are impressive just standing still. They have an air of authority, which the 6 is drawn to. A 6 will take notice and think: I really like this person, and maybe I could learn something from him. The 9 will respond to the 6's strength and ability to provide leadership and a beautiful environment. When they have children, the

9 will be impressed with the 6's legendary parenting skills. The 6 will blossom under the 9's open praise and appreciation. A partnership like this can last for a lifetime.

7–7: My observation of a 7 with a 7 is that they make great friends. They have a good time together; they enjoy each other's company. It's an excellent personal relationship, because they know when the other one is stressed; the 7 will listen to the 7 carefully and give advice, so there's a real feeling of comfort. Many Vibrations have difficulty with the 7's need for time alone, but nobody understands this need better than a fellow 7. They will never take it personally, but they have to work on keeping a physical connection. The mental connection's perfect; physical closeness can be lacking because of the loner quality of the 7. A perfect vacation for this couple would be an ocean cruise or a place where nature's beauty is everywhere, such as Hawaii or Tahiti. Writing or creating music together would be the ultimate career for the 7–7 couple.

7–8: In the beginning of the relationship, the 7-8 will be all over each other, because they actually rejuvenate each other in the bedroom. Nevertheless, it is important that the 8 try not to control the 7's life. The 7 will need a lot of sleep just to keep up with the 8. Since 8s tend to be workaholics, this can be okay with the 7 because they need their time alone. However, if children are involved, the 7 and 8 will have to work on being emotionally available to them. The 7 should leave the financial matters to the 8 because this is where they excel. If the 7s feel the 8s are always too busy for them, then they may need to find a way into the 8's business world. If the 7s shut down, and don't want to discuss what is upsetting them, flowers and cards saying how much they are really appreciated can do a world of good. The key to making this union last is for this couple to choose their words very carefully. Both are known for being too blunt. They must do everything they can to avoid unnecessary conflict.

7–9: The 7 and the 9 vibrations are considered Toxic to each other. However, when they are spiritual, that is to say, when the 7 believes in God, and does not act *like* they are God, the 9 will enjoy their company immensely. The first thing they will find they have in common is their need for intellectual stimulation.

This is a couple that may forget about other people because they get so locked into what they have to offer each other. Their minds can think as one. What can go wrong? When the 7 becomes too cynical and refuses to see the brighter side of a situation, the 9 will become frustrated with the 7, and eventually give up and want out. Another problem can be the 9 wallowing in old family issues, as they do when they are living in their negative energy. When this happens, the 7 will withdraw and not be there to comfort the 9. Supporting each other and really listening is what keeps this love strong. There can be peace and harmony here because a 7 and a 9 have so much going on that they both need space. They will be comfortable with the occasional absences of the other. When they get together again, they will really look forward to it and count themselves lucky for having such an understanding partner.

8–8: An 8 can do well with another 8 if they treat their relationship like a business. In this case, it would be the business of love. Respect what each other has to say, and make sure your fellow 8 knows how much they matter to you. I've always said an 8 Vibration can have trouble being with an 8 because they both learn the hard way. So when one is suffering, who consoles whom? It is especially important for the 8–8 couple to remember that the definition of insanity is "doing the same thing over and over again, and each time expecting a new result." Avoid going round and round in circles. You must also not be critical of each other. The 8s do not handle criticism well. Compromise is the key here, and then a solid partnership can result.

8–9: Although this is considered a Toxic number combination, it can work if the 8 is willing to respect the intelligence and wisdom that the 9 is blessed with. It is important that the 9 realize that although the 8 does not think in the same way, they do have a lot to offer. If the 8 is living on the negative side of its number, greed can get him or her into trouble. The 9 will not tolerate that kind of deception. When the 9 Life Path tries to enlighten the 8, it is important that they do not have a tone in their voice that could be interpreted as patronizing. If they do not watch their delivery, the 8 will lash out and really hurt the 9's feelings, often causing damage to the relationship that may be impossible to repair. When the 8 and 9 are at their best, they both have a strong desire to improve the world. They will volunteer their time, come up with a fund-raiser to help those in need, help find shelter for the homeless, etc. On this level, the world is a better place because they have found each another.

9–9: A 9 Life Path with a 9 Life Path is considered an excellent relationship because they are both here to make this a better world. They are usually involved with humanitarian issues. When they join forces, they are very impressive. These two will get things done. They have vast wisdom and knowledge, and constantly learn from each other. They're fascinated with each other's interpretation of life, which, interestingly enough, could be completely different. You are wondering, what could possibly go wrong? Well, the 9s mirror each other, so if they have a flaw, they will magnify it in their partner. They can spend a lifetime observing their parents and going over what went wrong. They have a desperate need to be perfect parents, and when they have children and something goes wrong (which it will), they can wallow in depression. It is essential that they forgive themselves for being human. The 9s are old souls, and they should have great respect for each other. They, unlike other number combinations, have a chance for a love that runs so deep, it transcends the merely physical and personal.

▪ MY THOUGHTS ON INFIDELITY ▪

No matter what your number, my belief is that if you have enough room in your marriage to have an affair, you should no longer be in that marriage. I say this because I believe that everyone has the right to be utterly and completely loved. I have clients who have told me, "We have not made love in five years," or, "We do nothing together and the best way for us to get along is to not talk at all." That is not living.

LADY DIANA—
17877, ATTITUDE 8

We had witnessed her in a sad and loveless marriage. She had been in all kinds of pain. She was finally coming into her own, getting strong, meeting a new man, and launching a crusade to end the crippling land mines that threaten so many defenseless people. The pictures taken before her death show a happy woman, working out in her gym, playing with her children. She was every one of us, trying to get on with her day-to-day life. And then, boom! She was pulled off the planet at age thirty-six.

For those of us who live with a chronic heartache, thinking, This man has never treated me right but maybe one day he will, or, I hate this job, but I need the money, one day I will look for another one, I say tomorrow may never come. God put us here for a reason. I think you need to pray every day. But if someone is verbally or physically abusive, you don't stay. No one deserves that. And if you're using someone for security, wake up. It's time for you to use your own gifts. The beauty of Numerology is to look at what your skills might be and take that chance, because God rewards people who have integrity. When you stay in a relationship that's a lie, there is no integrity.

▪ TAKING A LOOK AT PLATONIC RELATIONSHIPS ▪

Romance is only one type of relationship we encounter in life, and it's not the only place where compatibility is important. I recently discovered an example of this in my own life.

My office is in my home, which means it's a more intimate setting than the corporate world. When I hire people I try to pick those who will be responsible and get the job done, yet I have to keep an eye toward compatibility since what goes on in the office is hard to separate from what goes on at home. I concern myself primarily with my applicants' Life Path Numbers, looking for people who are Naturally Matched or a Compatible Number to my own.

But recently I hired someone whose Life Path was not compatible. I figured that after nearly two decades of studying numbers, I could overcome the challenges of a conflicting Life Path through sheer force of will. Unfortunately, I was wrong—and I learned my lesson the hard way. *When we feel a situation is out of control, no matter what our other numbers are, we will respond with the traits of our Life Path Number.* If our Life Path Numbers are in conflict, we're setting ourselves up for trouble.

My recent hire was someone I'd known peripherally for many years. For the sake of this story, we will call him Joe. Joe was a nice guy and needed a job. This was the first time that we would be working so closely together. I liked Joe very much, but I found we constantly disagreed. He fought me on everything and it seemed to amuse him.

I had known his Life Path was a Challenge to mine, but when things started to get really difficult I decided to look at the rest of his numbers. When I discovered he had five Challenge Numbers with me, *everything made sense!* Wow, when you invite someone with that many Challenge Numbers into your private life, you're setting yourself up to fail. As I said earlier in this chapter, when it comes to compatibility you need to look at the quantity of numbers in common—or in conflict. If you have one or two Challenge Numbers, you can overcome your differences. If you have three Challenge Numbers, you will always be working on your relationship. If you have four or five Challenge Numbers, you will feel a sense of depression and hopelessness about the relationship. That's where Joe and I had found ourselves.

Interestingly, there's another piece to this puzzle. Just a couple of years ago Joe actually had changed his name. Before the name change, he and I had *identical* Name Numbers. This not only gave us a Soul Mate Connection, but we found we had a lot of opinions about life that were exactly the same. When he made the change, all three numbers became Challenge Numbers to my name. We were no longer projecting the Natural Match energy that we once shared; our once-amazing rapport was now gone. Eventually, we had to part company to get our sanity back. I have no animosity toward him because Challenge Numbers run both ways.

While Joe and I were able to solve our differences by choosing not to work together anymore, such a solution is not always possible. In life we often have to find ways to coexist with people whose numbers challenge our own. This is where learning to understand people and their differences by the numbers becomes so crucial. Once you have a firm grasp of the numbers, you will be able to predict personality differences ahead of time and do what you can to prepare for them. And of course, when you're calling the shots—and doing the hiring—be sure to look at the numbers and hire compatible candidates whenever possible. That way you'll create a more productive, harmonious atmosphere where your employees will look forward to giving their best work.

Thirteen

The World Number

Now that you're more familiar with the power of numbers, you understand that every number in our lives carries a significant vibration. While we've covered the fact that the date you are born on sets the tone for your life, we haven't talked much about the role played by today's date. In fact, there are several ways today's date will impact your life. They are the World Number, the Personal Year, and the Personal Day. This chapter focuses on the World Number.

The World Number is the number that the current calendar year breaks down to. Let's look at 2005:

2005
2 + 5 = 7
2005 is a World Year of 7

The 7 year is a time to look inside you. It is not a time for widespread communication. If you are somebody who normally talks a lot, this year you might just want to write your thoughts down. If you are somebody who asks those big questions: "Who am I? What am I? Why am I here?" in this cycle of 7, you can get those answers. This year is a test of your faith; it is about true spirituality. You will grow inwardly in this cycle. We will be dealing with the seemingly endless conflicts in the Middle East, but looking at them in a different way.

This year is about raising our consciousness as a people, and realizing that the whole planet needs to treat each other as one. When one person dies, we all die a little. An irreplaceable part of the life chain is gone. The year of 7 is a time when we recognize that war is not an answer.

For those who have a base of faith, your most fervent prayers could be answered. For those who aren't sure if there is a God, this is the time to look into the possibility of a Higher Power. You are not alone. Listen to your heart. That quiet voice within can be made stronger by meditation, yoga, and being one with nature. Try to be outdoors more and especially near the water. By year's end we will have learned a lot about how connected we all are to each other as people, as well as to our wondrous planet. The world will come to understand the truth about violence: When we hurt somebody it's like a boomerang, it comes right back on us. In the World Year of 7, we will realize that we must take the steps toward a just and lasting peace. Our very survival depends on it.

▪ WHEN THE WORLD NUMBER IS THE SAME AS YOUR LIFE PATH: CATHERINE ZETA-JONES ▪

When the World Number coincides with your Life Path Number, the year can be an unusually powerful one for you. Let's look at someone whose life we're familiar with: actress Catherine Zeta-Jones.

> Catherine Zeta-Jones
> # 18975, Attitude 7

The year 2003 was a 5 year, because $2 + 0 + 0 + 3 = 5$. Catherine was born September 25, 1969, which breaks down to a 5 Life Path. This means 2003 was destined to be a memorable year in Catherine's life—which indeed it turned out to be! She received the Oscar for *Chicago,* she won a $1.6 million lawsuit with *Hello!* magazine for taking unauthorized photos of her at her wedding, and she gave birth to her second baby. On the night of the Oscars—eight months pregnant and looking radiant—she did a song and dance number with Queen Latifah that brought down the house. She also launched several lucrative spokesperson contracts, including T-Mobile and Elizabeth Arden. A pretty fantastic year, all told.

Because Catherine is so interesting from a Numerology perspective, let's go ahead and take a look at the rest of her chart while we're on the subject.

What motivates this incredibly driven woman? The answer lies in her 5 Life Path: The 5s need excitement in their lives. They get restless and they want to have multiple activities going on at once. Catherine also has an 8 in her name, which means financial stability matters a great deal to her. Both her reputation and her physical beauty are important to her, which is why she sued the magazine for publishing unflattering photos of her. One of the pictures showed her eating the wedding cake; she thought it made her look like a compulsive eater, an image that is completely unacceptable to her 5.

The number 5 is often compared to the cat. They have that graceful way of carrying their bodies, and their eyes are like magnets. Catherine Zeta-Jones is equally mesmerizing.

As for her relationship with Michael Douglas, the marriage makes perfect sense in terms of the numbers. Both she and Michael were born on September 25. When people born on the same day look at each other it's like looking into a mirror—there's an instant rapport and attraction. Michael Douglas has a 6 personality number, which is the father number. It's no surprise that one of the first things he said to Catherine when he met her was, "I want to be the father of your children." Two babies later, the couple is as happy as ever.

Naturally people gossip about their age difference. After all, 25 years is major. But interestingly, that's not a real concern to me. Instead, I'm concerned about the fact that Michael is a 7 Life Path to Catherine's 5. While these numbers are Naturally Matched, the 7 operates at a much slower pace than the 5. It would take a concerted effort for the 7 to keep up with the natural energy level of the 5. Here's where the age difference raises a flag: if this deficit of energy is true for 5s and 7s of the *same* age, what must it be like with a 25-year age difference? I would have to believe that as time goes on, it will become even more difficult for these two to coexist with each other for just this reason. It will be important for Catherine to keep herself extremely busy and not concern herself with the fact that Michael sometimes seems to be lagging behind. Catherine Zeta-Jones is a force to be reckoned with, and she will enchant us for many years to come.

▪ THE ROLE OF THE CENTURY ▪

The turn of the twenty-first century was an important one in terms of World Year. The century "19" was replaced by "20." Since 19 breaks down to a 1, while 20 breaks down to a 2, we left a century characterized by 1 traits and entered one characterized by the 2.

As we already know, the 1 can be selfish. So it's not surprising that we just left a hundred years of nations saying, "Me first." The great scourges of our day—poverty and war—were a direct result of this unwillingness to share. The world was saying, "Me first, you second . . . or not at all." The 1 stands alone, forgetting that it can be lonely at the top. Moreover, the 1 is independent, and in the latter half of the last century we saw couples struggling to stay married. "If I'm not happy," people were quick to say, "I'm out of here."

The year 2000 was a turning point, representing a shift in a much better direction. We're now in a century of 2. The 2 needs love. It's vulnerable, and not afraid to admit when something hurts. It takes us to a different level of truth, and gives over energy to love that had previously been focused on personal achievement. This century will also find an easing of the "real men don't cry" mentality. Men will be given greater freedom to express emotion, and the stereotype of the gruff, tough man will be softened.

There will be a lot more love in this century. The 2 craves unconditional love and wants to make things work, so this century will see an upswing in couples getting married and staying together. The 2 seeks harmony and peace, so we will learn in this century that war is not the answer. It's going to be wonderful to experience the rise of harmonious 2 energy, which will continue to grow over the next 100 years.

Fourteen

Getting Personal: Your Personal Years, Months, and Days

Now that we understand the concept of the World Number, let's talk about a year number that's closer to home. This is your Personal Year Number, which is found by combining the World Year Number with the month and date of your birth.

▪ PERSONAL YEAR NUMBER ▪

As you should now know, the number that comes from the month and date of your birth is your Attitude Number. So, the way we discover your Personal Year Number is:

World Year Number + Attitude Number = Personal Year Number

Let's look at the actor Bill Murray, who had a phenomenal year in 2004. Murray's birthday is 9/21/1950, making him an Attitude 3. In the last section we broke down 2004 and saw that it was a World Year 6. So,

6 + 3 = 9

Bill Murray had a Personal Year of 9 in 2004.

In a Personal Year of 9, you will get some sort of payoff for all of your efforts accumulated from the last nine years. In 2004, Bill won the Golden Globe for best actor in the comedy/musical division—it was his second nomination but his first win. The movie, *Lost in Translation*, was widely acclaimed by both critics and fans. Bill has reached the peak of a very successful career that had taken him from comedy, to romance, to drama, and on to his latest effort, which was a compilation of all three genres. Since Bill was in his Personal Year of 9, it was so appropriate that he was finally acknowledged for being such a brilliant talent. Let's take a more in-depth look at Bill Murray by looking at all of his numbers, which are 41539 Attitude 3.

His chart makes it very clear why Bill Murray is such a successful comic actor. He was born on a 3 day, which means he appears as the comedian; and he has a 3 Attitude, someone always looking for the punch line. The Number 3 is the natural comedian. The numbers 3, 6, and 9 belong in front of the camera; this man has a double 3 *and* a 9 in his birth chart.

Some people make you laugh as soon as you see them. Bill Murray is one of those people; but this man has been through a lot to get where he is. There's nothing funny about the hard work he's put in to get where he is today. Still, he keeps the audience laughing. He made a very funny acceptance speech at the night of the Golden Globes. He said, "I would like to thank all the people at Focus and Universal, but because there are so many people taking credit for the success of this film, I wouldn't know where to begin."

Bill's affinity for hard work is also borne out by his chart. He has a 4 as his Soul Number, which is the hard lesson number—meaning he is diligent, but also that he has his ups and downs. There was a time in his career, in the late 1980s, where he went into a depression for four years and took time out from his larger ambitions, and just did a series of small roles, because he was mentally taxed.

His Personality Number is a 1, which means he strives to be the winner. In the book *Audition: Everything an Actor Needs to Know to Get the Part*, Michael Shurtleff says, "Comedy is rarely based on kindness. It is based on cutthroat competitiveness." This is exactly true for Bill Murray. His wit is biting and sardonic, but executed with such finesse that you can't help but laugh. The 1 shows his need to compete and win. The name Bill Murray adds up to a Power Name Number 5; electricity surrounds this man, you can feel it at once.

Bill's 9 Life Path means he has issues stemming from his original family. He came from a family of eight brothers and one sister, who became a nun. The kids used to compete to get the attention of the father. One of the things they would do is imitate their overworked mother—with no one laughing harder than she.

One story that's been written about Bill is that he was doing a James Cagney impression on top of the dinner table, and he fell off the table and cracked his head hard on the table's metal foot. It no doubt hurt badly, but when he looked up and saw his father laughing hysterically, he couldn't help laughing and crying at the same time.

His need for applause was strong, and in a big family you get your attention at almost any cost. (Believe me, I know what I'm talking about—I'm from a family of eleven, and I have a double 3 in my birth numbers, so I really relate to Mr. Murray!)

As we all witnessed in the year of 2004, Bill is finally getting the acknowledgment he so deserves. To quote Dominic Wills: "Many actors can be said to have come a long way, but Bill Murray's track to serious recognition has been a truly epic journey. As a great comedian and now a fine actor he deserves all the praise he gets."

▪ PERSONAL YEAR NUMBER DESCRIPTIONS ▪

Personal Year of 1: When it's your Personal Year of 1, it's time to be number one at what you do. The year before, you were in the Personal Year of 9, of clearing, of getting everything ready. Now in the Personal Year of 1 it's time to reap the benefits! It's your turn to be the best at what you do and for people to look up to you as a leader. It's your moment to have the credibility you deserve. Whether it's business or love, you can go after it and achieve it in that Personal Year of 1.

Personal Year of 2: Think of this as a year to work on your emotional side. Let's say you were so caught up in work in during your previous year (a year of 1) that by the Personal Year of 2 you're ready to look at love. It's time to work on intimacy and relationships. Make sure you haven't neglected your partner because you've been so caught up achieving the big dream. The Personal Year of 2 is about affection, spending time with someone you care about and sharing your real feelings. It's a year to let your guard down, not be afraid to say "I love and need you." You'll find it rewarding to discuss your emotional side. Your Personal Year of 2 is the right time to take that vacation your loved one has been pressing for—to really appreciate those you care about by fostering healthy, loving relationships.

Personal Year of 3: The Personal Year of 3 is the time to look at your creative side. If you're a singer who never sings, it's time to go to a karaoke bar. If you never acted but thought you could, take an acting class. This year is all about expression, dressing up, being more glamorous, taking a chance, going to a restaurant you normally feel you can't afford, turning your humdrum life into a romantic, magical place. Living your life in a big way: That's the Personal Year of 3. A sense of humor is important because the 3 is the clown. If you're a normally quiet, introspective number—a 7 Life Path number, for instance— you'll find yourself opening up and talking more in your Personal Year of 3. If you're married to a 7 who tends to be quiet, when that Personal Year of 3 comes up, know that there is more of a chance he or she is going to be verbally receptive to you.

Personal Year of 4: The 4 is the expert, so this is the year to sharpen your skills. If you're a cerebral person, this is the year to read books. Let's say you're very good at baseball; maybe this is the year you become a coach. If there's something you're good at, start using your skills, because this is the year to let other people benefit from your knowledge. The Personal Year of 4 brings a need for home life too; this is a good time to upgrade from that apartment you've never liked to owning your own home with a yard. Start putting a plan together for your future and begin living it today.

Personal Year of 5: It's a whirlwind life when you're in a Personal Year of 5. Your energies are scattered; the things you try to make happen tend not to pan out. If you're about to buy a house, you may find that it falls through. You might have agreed to transfer to a new job 3,000 miles away and you'll get a call saying they don't actually need you for another six months. These are the ups and downs of the Personal Year of 5, and you just have to take it in stride. If nothing stays put in a 5 year, what's the best approach? Just keep moving! It's the time to travel if you can. Get out in the world; run and embrace everything you can on this planet. At the same time, this isn't a year to be making commitments. If you've met someone and think you're madly in love, please wait 'til the end of the year before you tie the knot! I've heard too many stories from women who have been burned by love in a Personal Year of 5. One client had a one-night stand, and found she was pregnant. Another thought she had met the man of her dreams—before she discovered the guy was a major drug addict. So in this Personal Year of 5 it's best to catch movies, read fascinating books, and find ways to keep your sanity. And when things seem to be getting out of hand, remember this phrase: "This too shall pass."

Personal Year of 6: The Personal Year of 6 is the year to get married or have a child. If you meet someone and get married in this year, it's a very solid time to do it. After the crazy Personal Year of 5, you're ready to settle down! The 6 is the interior decorator, and I've found that people in their Personal Year of 6 look at their home and say, "Okay, it's time to redo this. Let's repaint, let's redesign the kitchen." It is time to look at your surroundings and do something different. In a Personal Year of 6 you don't feel comfortable being bossed around or told what to do; you may even get the urge to start your own company. The 6 will also create a magnetic power drawing people to you. If you're the kind of person who prefers to be ignored, you're going to have to deal with being the focus of attention in your Personal Year of 6. Chances are your intuitions are correct at this time—I would trust myself in a 6 year. Contracts may come your way, because people suddenly want to close a deal with you. Big opportunities arise after the bizarre Personal Year of 5, where nothing made sense. People mean what they say and come through for you in the Personal Year of 6.

Personal Year of 7: In a Personal Year of 7, your faith is going to be tested. You look at your life and say, "Oh my God, I can't believe this happened." If you are a truly spiritual person, chances are you feel it on a very deep level. It tends to be emotional. You wind up questioning everything: "Is there a God?" "What am I doing here?" This is a time of introspection. I recommend browsing metaphysical bookstores and investigating religion and spirituality. This is also the year to look into counseling or therapy. Although you may just want to be alone with your thoughts, sometimes a counselor can help walk you through the toughest parts and help you really grow. In a Personal Year of 7, you need to get near the water (even if it's just a Jacuzzi) because being in water will focus your energies. You need to nurture and love yourself, especially if you're not in a relationship. I would also say that in a Personal Year of 7 it's hard to talk to your partner. You may be experiencing inner turmoil, but it's about you and not them. Be sure to make an effort to be open and clear so they don't think they've done something wrong.

Personal Year of 8: Money can come to you in abundance in the Personal Year of 8. Financially providing for your family seems to take priority over communicating with them this year, so make sure to go out of your way to let them know you love them. In the Personal Year of 8, you should be working, making a living, establishing security, and getting the job done. This is a good year to start investing, because the Energy will be on your side. It's the year to master your income. When you're in the Personal Year of 8 you have to be careful not to be insensitive to the feelings of others while achieving your dreams. You may feel verbally attacked or overly criticized by some of the people in your life. Do not take it personally. It is their problem. Just make sure you're still conveying warmth and love to those around you, and everything will fall into place. If you make this conscious effort, you can get ahead personally, as well as in your career, in this 8 Personal Year.

Personal Year of 9: When you are in the 9 Personal Year, you look at your life and say, "Wait a second, what's going on? What's worth saving? What isn't? What should go?" If you have possessions that have not been glanced at for six months, or more, let them go. You can finally clear it away when you enter the 9 Personal Year. It is the time to clean the closet, make new choices, and make room for the good stuff that's coming. It's also when you make important phone calls—you will definitely get through. And when you make phone calls and try to make things happen, there are a lot of green lights in the Year of 9. You find that you can get past the secretary! And all those plans you had that never came together? In the Personal Year of 9 they do!

▪ YOUR PERSONAL MONTH ▪

To determine what Personal Month you are in, take your Personal Year Number and add it to the present month. And the number you come up with is the Personal Month you are in.

For example, someone born May 5, 1952, would be in their Personal Year of 8 in 2005 (World Number 7).

Here's why:

Add the month and day, which is $5 + 5 = 10 = 1 + 0 = 1$
Take the 1 and add it to the World Number 7, which equals 8.
$1 + 7 = 8$

Your Personal Year Number is 8. Add 8 to the present month number, and you will have the number of your Personal Month.

Here are examples:

July: $7 + 8 = 15 = 1 + 5 = 6$
= 6 Personal Month
August: $8 + 8 = 16 = 1 + 6 = 7$
= 7 Personal Month
September: $9 + 8 = 17 = 1 + 7 = 8$
= 8 Personal Month

▪ PERSONAL MONTH DESCRIPTIONS ▪

Personal Month of 1: This is the time to become more independent. Learn to deal with your problems. You can ask for help in figuring things out, but don't expect others to take on the problem. This is a great month to accomplish your goals, sign contracts, and nurture any new venture. Travel is also good in this month. This is a fine time to end a bad association, business or personal.

Personal Month of 2: This is a month to relax in. Not a month for new adventures, it's a good time to look up old friends, and stick with the tried and true. People are very willing to help you now. Let them. Avoid gloomy thoughts. Focus on your love life. Let's say you're a 1 Life Path and you're used to being number one. This is the month to kick back and relax, to just observe for a change.

Personal Month of 3: What's a 3 month? High energy and having a good time. Going to a show, to a party, anything where you're being more playful. I would say the more serious numbers like the 4 Life Path and 7 Life Path, which can get intense, would have to let their inner child come out and play in the month of 3.

Personal Month of 4: Now is the time to finish any task you've been putting off. Balance your checkbook, repaint your house, and prune your rosebushes. Get your financial records straight. You'll be more efficient this month, and these tasks, tedious at other times, seem much easier. Make sure everything is handled, everyone is taken care of. It would be wise to take a look at the personal issues you have been neglecting in the Personal Month of 4.

Personal Month of 5: Many of the things that happen in this month will be gone by the next. Not a month to enter into long-term agreements. People will seem fickle; your own emotions are subject to change. Keep it light; do not lose your sense of humor. It's an excellent time to throw a party or go on a weekend trip. The best way to deal with the 5 month is to pretend it's an action-packed movie—grab your bag of popcorn and just watch it go by.

Personal Month of 6: This is the month to decorate the house. Romance is great now, and new acquaintances can turn into lasting friendships. It's a good time to end a disillusioning romantic entanglement. Family is most important now. Call the relative or friend you've been neglecting. A 6 month would be the time to get back to the basics, family and home.

Personal Month of 7: Much of life seems to be a struggle against time—so much to do and so little time to do it in. This month gives you a little breather. Sit back and look inside yourself—take stock. Even if you're a party animal, you may find a need to be alone. Heed the feeling, it's your inner wisdom speaking. Live simply, purify your diet, and try not to overdo alcohol. Be calm and stay centered. In your 7 month, if you're near a beach, get to it, read a book there, look at the ocean. Appreciate nature. Climb a mountain, go river rafting. This is the month to experience and appreciate the beauty of the planet. It's a time to be introspective and write down your thoughts. Concentrate on your affirmations.

Personal Month of 8: It's a good time to look at your finances, and be extra careful with money. Start a savings account. Watch out for the loss of your keys, keepsakes, or objects that are meaningful to you. In this month, people can be scattered and may make some mistakes. Avoid getting into an argument, you could lose a good friend. No one is perfect and this is a month to really keep that in mind.

Personal Month of 9: This is a good time to make some changes, get rid of the clothes you don't wear. Throw away papers you no longer need. Take your old books to the Goodwill or a secondhand bookstore. This is also a great month to move. The 9 enjoys being charitable. This month give to public TV (the envelope is where you put it six months ago), or perhaps join a food drive. The decisions you make during your 9 month will make you feel better for the rest of the year.

▪ LIVING EACH DAY BY THE NUMBERS:
THE 31-DAY CALENDAR ▪

I am often asked whether there are particular days that are more auspicious than others for a particular person to make big decisions, travel, have a serious discussion with a loved one, or even take a day off. The answer is a resounding *yes!* There are particular days out of every month that are naturally *favorable* to your Life Path Number. If the day of the month breaks down to your Life Path Number or a number that is *Naturally Matched* to your Life Path, then that day is considered one of the best days for you. The vibration of that particular day is on your side.

Let's look at an example. If you are a 3 Life Path, then any day that breaks down to a 3 is a positive day for you. Moreover, the numbers that are Naturally Matched to the 3 are 3, 6, and 9—so any days that break down to those numbers will be favorable for you as well. (To refresh yourself on the Natural Match Numbers, look at the list beginning on page 18.)

It is wise to make all the big moves in your life on a Compatible or Naturally Matched day. Things you might consider doing on these days include scheduling your wedding, closing on a home, moving, signing an important contract, or going on a job interview.

The 1st of the Month: This is a 1 day. Find a way to feel like a winner. Buy a new outfit, or go to a good restaurant for dinner. Call a friend and go play a sport you really enjoy such as tennis, bike riding, golf, etc. It is definitely a day to get some physical release. If you are in a relationship that is causing you pain, this is a good day to end it. If you have been thinking about quitting your job, this would be the day to pick up the Classifieds. It is all about you getting into the driver's seat of your life!!

This is a particularly favorable day for a 1, 5, and 7.

The 2nd of the Month: This is a 2 day. This day is about friendship, peace, and harmony; try to spend it with a loved one. If there is someone that you truly care for, pick up the phone and make a plan. Send flowers to a friend just to make their day. Listen to music that makes you happy. Treat yourself to a massage. If you are fighting with someone, this is the day to come to an agreement. Avoid emotional vampires who are out to steal your joy. Give them your best smile, and keep on moving.

This is a particularly favorable day for a 2, 4, and 8.

The 3rd of the Month: This is a 3 day. Seize every opportunity for self-expression. Surround yourself with fun people who are in touch with their inner child. Go dancing, karaoke, to the movies, etc. Today is all about embracing the creative side of life. Do something kind for a perfect stranger. Only good can come from it. Find ways to laugh. If you have a favorite old comedy tape, pop it into your VCR. This is also a great day to sell something. If you have an idea you have wanted to pitch to your boss, this is the right time to do it. Don't be surprised if you get a bonus or raise out of it!

This is a particularly favorable day for a 3, 6, and 9.

The 4th of the Month: This is a 4 day. It is a perfect day to get caught up on all of your bills. If you have let the housework go, this is also an ideal day for cleaning. Try to learn something new. Pick up that book you've wanted to read. Whatever you do, avoid confrontations. People love to argue on a 4 day, and it is really a waste of time. If you are normally outspoken, bite your tongue. You will definitely regret what you say if you don't!

This is a particularly favorable day for a 2, 4, and 8.

The 5th of the Month: This is a 5 day. It could be a lucky day for you—take a chance, like playing the lottery. Do something special for yourself. Get a massage, buy a new outfit, get your hair done, etc. If you could get a group of friends together for a spontaneous dinner, you are sure to have a blast. Do not bother trying to control this day. It will lead you. This is not a day for big decisions. If you act rashly, you will be sorry later. You could solve a mystery at work or regarding your family. This is a definite day for the detective in you to come out and play!

This is a particularly favorable day for a 1, 5, and 7.

The 6th of the Month: This is a 6 day. If you normally are on the go, today is a day to stay at home. Take a close look at what is going on within your family.

If you are single, pick up the phone and chat with someone you have been neglecting. You will be more sensitive to smell and sight today. Look at your surroundings. Is it time to make some changes? Even buying a little something for your home or apartment will make you feel much better. Listen to some calming music. Pick up a scented candle for some aromatherapy. It will definitely make you feel better.

This is a particularly favorable day for a 3, 6, and 9.

The 7th of the Month: This is a 7 day. You should take time out today to study, learn, and seek the truth. Spend time on your own. Get with nature, the ocean, mountains, etc. If you are usually a big communicator, stay quiet and just observe. On the other hand, if you are normally quiet, this is the day to speak your mind. If you are troubled by a problem in your life, light a white candle, shut your eyes, and ask your inner voice what you should do. The answer will come to you.

This is a particularly favorable day for a 1, 5, and 7.

The 8th of the Month: This is an 8 day. You should work on a specific goal and stay focused. Watch your money, or you could make a financial investment that you will regret. Be open to advice, and pay close attention to your driving. Unfortunately, it is very common to get a speeding ticket or in some sort of accident on an 8 day. Keep your sense of humor and avoid any confrontations. Life is too short for unnecessary battles.

This is a particularly favorable day for a 2, 4, and 8.

The 9th of the Month: This is a 9 day. If you have been avoiding dealing with a negative family scenario, this is the day to take care of it. This is also a day to take the lead in any situation at work or at home. You will be rewarded for taking the initiative. If there is an important call you have been putting off, this is the day to make it. Choose your words carefully, and it will all work out in your favor. Today you need to demonstrate all the tolerance and understanding that you have learned. This is a day to make a new friend and visit new places. If you set a personal goal today, you will definitely achieve it!

This is a particularly favorable day for 3, 6, and 9.

The 10th of the Month: The 10th is a 1 day. Do not waste a moment, because this is a day of opportunity and you may not be given a second chance. Be positive, do something active, and face up to any problems that have been worrying you recently. If you want to get physically fit, this is the day to hire a personal trainer. If you need to get a project completed, call on an expert to help you achieve excellence. Action is your key word here.

This is a particularly favorable day for a 1, 5, and 7.

The 11th of the Month: The 11th breaks down to a 2, but is also a Master Number. Leave materialism behind you. The vibrations today are highly attuned and very spiritual. Your intuition is strong. Do not force anything, and be silent. Make an effort to keep the peace. Let the day flow and make sure you arrive right on time wherever you go. Don't force your opinion on anyone. Be a pure light today because you can truly inspire the people you come into contact with.

This is a particularly favorable day for a 2, 4, and 8.

The 12th of the Month: The 12th is a 3 day—a particularly lucky day. You should get out and about and generally have a good time. There's plenty to be done, but you should have more than enough energy to cope with anything today and still find time for fun. If you are at work today, definitely make plans with a best friend for lunch. Be playful with your partner. Tonight is all about sensuality and passion.

This is a particularly favorable day for a 3, 6, and 9.

The 13th of the Month: The 13th is a 4 day, meaning that today is not a day to look for excitement. A 4 day can be rather routine. Be practical; get all your chores done now. Read a good book. Balance your checkbook. If it is Friday the 13th, do not give any energy to the idea of having bad luck. It can be a day of learning a difficult lesson, but if you *really* learn that lesson, it will be well worth it!

This is a particularly favorable day for a 2, 4, and 8.

The 14th of the Month: This is a 5 day, a day full of surprises. Anything is possible. Today will exude a sense of excitement and adventure. Dress to impress. If you are a woman, take the extra time needed for your hair and makeup. If you're a guy, make an effort to look impressive. This will keep everybody guessing, and oh what fun you'll have. Be spontaneous and take a chance. Go to a restaurant or a part of town you have never been to. If there is someone in the office that you have had your eye on, ask him or her out. This is a day to take a gamble, and see what happens!

This is a particularly favorable day for a 1, 5, and 7.

The 15th of the Month: The 15th is a 6 day. If you have had a falling out, or perhaps have argued with your partner recently, then now is the time to bury the hatchet and say you're sorry. Any conflicts can be reconciled today. This is also a favorable day for social gatherings, meetings, or for just visiting friends.

This is a particularly favorable day for a 3, 6, and 9.

The 16th of the Month: This is a 7 day, when you should seek peace and quiet far away from people and distractions. You need some time on your own to meditate or just think things over. It is also a good day for those of you involved in study or research. For relaxation, get in the water. Whether it is the ocean, swimming pool, or simply a long shower, it will help clear your mind and give you a feeling of serenity.

This is a particularly favorable day for a 1, 5, and 7.

The 17th of the Month: An 8 day, this is a good day in terms of finance or large-scale business plans. You should make a constructive effort to produce something tangible today. Pay close attention to details, no matter how small. Be open to advice. Start a journal and make a list of what it will take to achieve your personal goals. The perfect quote to sum up today would be: "If you want more, make yourself worth more!"

This is a particularly favorable day for a 2, 4, and 8.

The 18th of the Month: This 9 day is a positive day. A day of personal satisfaction coupled with fulfilled ambitions. Do something special for your family. They will really appreciate it. Release all that no longer benefits you—ideas, habits, and relationships. If you have some things in your home that you have wanted to get rid of, today is the day. Throw things out or give them to the Goodwill. You will not regret it.

This is a particularly favorable day for a 3, 6, and 9.

The 19th of the Month: On this 1 day, be independent. Do what you want to do. Go to unfamiliar places. Meet innovative people. Try out new ideas. This is a good day for a job interview, especially one involving a leadership position. To relieve stress, make an effort to get some exercise. Trust yourself and your intuition. Be original, creative, and ambitious. Don't let anger or impatience sabotage your efforts. This is a day to embrace your personal power.

This is a particularly favorable day for a 1, 5, and 7.

The 20th of the Month: Be peaceful on this 2 day. This is a day to be especially agreeable. Do more than your fair share. Go above and beyond. Volunteer your services at the charity of your choice. If you are normally a talker, then this is a day to just listen. Be patient and diplomatic. Observe, and write down your thoughts. Take the time to put others at ease, and be aware of their feelings. Today you have the power to experience true serenity.

This is a particularly favorable day for a 2, 4, and 8.

The 21st of the Month: The 21st is a 3 day—laugh and have fun today! People are especially important. It's a social day. Sing, dance, and play. You need to express yourself. Today is all about the joy of living. Look your best and feel good about yourself. Experience the joy that is in you, and share it with others. Let your creativity express itself freely. This is a great day for shopping—find that special gift for the one you love.

This is a particularly favorable day for a 3, 6, and 9.

The 22nd of the Month: The 22nd day breaks down to a 4, and is also a Master Number day. Forget yourself and your own interests. Strive for today to be selfless. You must find ways to make a positive difference for everyone. If you do something that only benefits you, it will backfire. The bigger your generous gesture, the more you will be rewarded karmically. Think of clever ways to make a difference. You'll be surprised by how much joy it will bring you.

This is a particularly favorable day for a 2, 4, and 8.

The 23rd of the Month: A 5 day, this is a perfect day to solve a personal mystery. In other words, if you want to find out the truth about someone or something that has been troubling you, this is the day to play detective. Try being flexible. A 5 day is an excellent day to travel or throw a party. Catch the latest movie or go shopping. This is not a day to stay home and be inactive. If you must stay home, read a thrilling book or watch TV.

This is a particularly favorable day for a 1, 5, and 7.

The 24th of the Month: On this 6 day, take a personal inventory. Look at your house. Could you make it more comfortable? How about yourself? Could you be more polished? Review your diet. Does it need adjusting? Look at your personality. Could it be more cheerful? Look at your responsibilities. Are you caught up on all of your responsibilities? Are you sticking your nose into other people's business? If so, let it go. Do you owe anyone money? This is the day to make payment arrangements. Stay home. Enjoy your family and entertain them. Fill your day with music. This is also a wonderful day for moving into a new home.

This is a particularly favorable day for a 3, 6, and 9.

The 25th of the Month: As a 7 day, this is a day to be alone, at least for part of the day. Be still. Read. Think. Listen to your inner soul. Drop the business world. If you pursue money today, it will elude you. If you keep still and wait, things will come to you. Study something spiritual or scientific. Take a long walk or a drive in the country. The number 7 always reveals something. Meditate. Be open to a personal message from the universe.

This is a particularly favorable day for a 1, 5, and 7.

The 26th of the Month: On this 8 day, ambition stirs within you. It's a time for advancement. Look and act successful. The 8 day is a strong business day.

Act like an executive when accessing your life. Organize and reorganize. Use good judgment. Pay your bills. Do all your financial and legal work. This is the best day for signing leases or contracts. Go to the gym or have a health checkup. This is not a day to park somewhere illegally "for just a second" and think you won't get a ticket—you will.

This is a particularly favorable day for a 2, 4, and 8.

The 27th of the Month: The entire world is your family on this 9 day. Be caring. Help everyone you can. Give something away. Be generous and kind. No beginnings today; finish up things. Go for completion. Clean out closets and drawers. If you don't use something you own, give it away or sell it. Use your creative talents. A great day for public performance. What you give out will come back to you, so give only the best.

This is a particularly favorable day for a 3, 6, and 9.

The 28th of the Month: If you are in an unhappy relationship, this is the day to give an ultimatum. You really do not need to put up with any kind of abuse. If you feel things are not right, then it is time to speak up and say something. This would apply to business and financial matters as well. This is also a day to do some buying or selling. It is a day of movement—definitely not a day to procrastinate!

This is a particularly favorable day for 1, 5, and 7.

The 29th of the Month: The 29th is a 2 day, a day for thoughts and plans rather than for actions. Think over your problems and how best to solve them. Do not enter into any form of agreement today, whether a verbal promise or a signed contract. Instead, work out all the details so that you are clear about what you are getting yourself into. If you are in a relationship or just going out with someone for the first time, this is a wonderful night for romance.

This is a particularly favorable day for a 2, 4, and 8.

The 30th of the Month: It's a 3 day today, and laughter is the best medicine! Don't take anything or anyone too seriously. Call a former classmate to share old funny memories. If you have been out of touch with someone you value, this is the day to play catch-up. Do something silly. Take a dance class, watch a classic comedy movie, or dress up and hit the town. You will be noticed today, so why not be the star that you are!

This is a particularly favorable day for a 3, 6, and 9.

The 31st of the Month: The 31st is a 4 day, and this is a good day to get up early and really seize the day. Grab a cup of coffee and, if possible, watch the sun rise. Nature's beauty will have a profound effect on you today. Get going on those unfinished projects. Pay your bills. Write those letters. Balance the budget. Be organized and dependable. Do your repairs. The work you do today will really make a difference and get you ready for a brand-new month.

This is a particularly favorable day for a 2, 4, and 8.

Fifteen

Naming by the Numbers

You're familiar with the Pythagorean chart now, so you know that the numbers vibrate through the letters of the alphabet, and are especially important when it comes to your name. Your name can actually make a difference in your personality, and unlike your birth numbers, this is something you can control.

You'll find throughout your life that choosing names is very important to you—if you're a parent, you name your child; if you're a business owner, you name your business; if you're an author, you name your book. Each of these choices has implications for those people and things that you have named. Read on to find out how you can use this power to your advantage.

▪ THE ALPHABET AND THE FIRST VOWEL ▪

Every letter has a numerical value. I believe in keeping this information simple. Take your first name, for example. It is true that every letter in your name vibrates with a different energy, and there is a lot of information you can learn from studying each one of those letters.

But in the interest of simplicity, I suggest looking most closely at the first vowel. The first vowel is especially important because that's the vibration that will resonate in your soul for your entire life. The second thing I would look at is the name's Intensity Number, or the number that comes up most often when you break down the letters. (For more about the Intensity Number, see chapter 11.)

▪ THE FIRST VOWEL IN YOUR NAME ▪

The first vowel in your first name tells us what is true for you inside. It's something you're always going to feel. If I meet someone whose name is Bob, I'm going to ask, "Bob, do you have kids?" The O in his name is the 6, the parent number. You'd be shocked how often it is the case. If I meet a David, I know instantly that this person is self-motivated, a hard worker, someone you don't have to keep tabs on—David will definitely get the job done. This is because the A is a 1 vibration. This is knowledge instantly gained from the first name; you don't even have to know someone's birthday to have this insight.

THE Y FACTOR

Remember that a Y counts as a vowel if it's next to a consonant (on both sides), a consonant if it's next to a vowel (on either side). For instance:

KENNE*D Y*—It comes next to the consonant D, so in this case Y counts as a vowel.

YUL BRENNER—It comes next to the vowel U, so in this case the Y counts as a consonant.

What this means in terms of choosing a name is that you should try your best to make sure the Power Name Number is a Natural Match or Compatible Number with the Life Path. Remember, when you give a child a name you are helping to form his character. There is more about baby names later in this chapter.

▪ FIRST VOWEL DESCRIPTIONS—A, E, I, O, U ▪

First Vowel A

- Vibration: 1
- Example: MARY
- Characteristic: Independence

A's are solid, sturdy people who seek honesty, truth, and wisdom. The first vowel, the A, or 1, is a hard worker. They do a great job, but if they make even one mistake, they feel they have failed. If you say to the A, "You're doing great," they continue to give you greatness. If you criticize them, they will rebel. I know if there is a Mary reading this, she'll say: "Oh my God, that's me!"

So when you meet a person whose first vowel is an A, think, This person is independent.

Mary Tyler Moore
Sandra Bullock
Armand Assante

First Vowel E

- Vibration: 5
- Example: ELAINE
- Characteristic: Need for freedom to celebrate life

E's believe in beauty; they want to bring magic to our planet. They are the detectives and like to uncover the mystery. They are often fascinated by Numerology because of their love of people. If they saw a homeless woman, they would want to know her story. Unfortunately for them, since E's are lights, they often attract bugs! Elaine might get drained if she takes on the wrong people. The E likes to look good, and wants the people around them to look good too. They have a critical eye. The goal of the E is to never have an unexciting moment. They hate to feel trapped or controlled. Free expression is everything to them.

A famous example would be Ellen DeGeneres. Not only did she come out, she decided to come out on her show in front of 36 million people. Talk about turning your real life into a soap opera that no one would want to miss!

Drew Barrymore
Elvis Presley
Eva Péron

First Vowel I

- Vibration: 9
- Example: B*I*LL
- Characteristic: Leaders with residual family history

The I is a 9, and has issues with family. This may mean the I feels unloved or abandoned, or perhaps feels an exceptional amount of responsibility for his or her parents. Sometimes these people with the I energy were adopted, physically abused, or lost a parent at a young age.

An example is Bill Clinton, whose father died shortly before his birth. Bill is very open about an incident in which he protected his mother from an attack by his stepfather; this is exactly what an I would do. The I would not have been able to stand by and watch that happen.

The I vibration is the natural leader. People assume they're in charge even if they're not. They're the kind of people we want to look up to.

Ivana Trump
Billie Jean King
Rita Hayworth

First Vowel O

- Vibration: 6
- Example: DONNA
- Characteristic: Should be the one in charge

O is the 6 energy. O's usually have children, and if they don't have children, they usually have pets that they baby. They don't do well working for others, and should always be in a position of authority. O's can't have people controlling them or watching them too closely. They'll give you the benefit of the doubt, but if you betray them, they are unforgiving. They feel the need to protect people in their lives but sometimes feel like it's a thankless position. The saying "If Mama ain't happy, ain't nobody happy" applies here. The O is magnetic and if they're not happy, they can send a serious chill through a room.

A celebrity example is Oprah Winfrey. She's the biggest O of all—the mother of what? America! She doesn't have kids, but she mothers all of us, and she does it well. She's got the incredible competence characteristic of the O, and she runs her company Harpo Productions just like the O would.

Rosie O'Donnell
Mother Teresa
John Kennedy

First Vowel U

- Vibration: 3
- Example: JUDITH
- Characteristic: Storytellers who live a colorful lifestyle

The U is the communicator; they tell stories beautifully. Little kids with U energy will often be breathless with excitement over the stories they have to tell you! Even adult U's are in touch with their inner children, so they make great comedians. They are animated and excited; they're out of breath—they just can't wait to tell you. When the U energy lights up and smiles, they're beautiful, they're not just attractive. If they're gloomy it's like a rainy day; they really have that ability to manipulate the room. The reason U encourages comedy is that they are in touch with their inner child at all times.

I will say it's a very extreme energy. U's are spontaneous, they don't think; they just do it and later they pay the consequences. They're definitely in the moment. U's try to fill in their day with excitement. If the U is not using that energy in a creative way, they exaggerate the truth just to make it sound more interesting.

Actress Julie Andrews once revealed that as a child, she kept a diary. But because her real family life was so unpleasant, she filled her book instead with tales of a charmed life, complete with a fire crackling in the fireplace and joyful holiday celebrations. She explained that she had written these fictional accounts so that in case anyone found the diary, they would think this was the truth.

You won't be able to have that U vowel and not be able to give great advice; it's the counselor number. Communication is essential.

Justin Timberlake
Julia Roberts
Lucille Ball

First Vowel Y

- Vibration: 7
- Example: GWYNETH
- Characteristic: Wise beyond their years and often have spiritual issues

The Y energy is opinionated; when Y's make a decision, it's impossible to change their minds. The Y energy doesn't want you to know exactly what's going on with them. They know how to keep a secret and if they decide they've really been burned, they are grudge holders.

The Y energy needs to be around nature; the ocean really has a calming effect on them. Y's are intelligent; they have mental and spiritual power. It's an incredibly strong energy if they use it correctly, but if they don't, it can be destructive. When in the positive, the Y is optimistic, but on the flip side they can be cynical. They have a lethal tongue and if they decide to tear you down, you will feel very small when they are through.

I think this is true about anyone who has a healing energy. If you have a healing energy, you can flip it. (After all, the devil started out as an angel, didn't he?) Pythagoras added a Y to his name to feel the energy and spirituality of the Y (7). He wanted to experience the difference it would make in his life.

Tyra Banks
Gypsy Rose Lee
Tyrone Power

▪ BABY NAMES ▪

If I were an expectant mother thinking about baby names, how would I use Numerology to welcome this new member of the family? Obviously, you cannot predict the day that your baby is going to be born. (Unless you opt to induce or have a C-section . . . my joke is that I'd rather have a C-section than give birth to a Toxic number!) Truth is, it really doesn't matter what your child's birth date is. Even if he or she has a Life Path that is not compatible with yours, the fact that you've studied the numbers and understand what motivates each number means that you won't take your differences so much to heart.

At the same time, since you have control over the child's name, it's in your best interest to pick a name that has as many numbers of yours as possible. That way, you have an even better chance of having three out of five numbers in common—a Soul Mate Connection with your child. When you pick a name, you should look for birth name numbers that are a Natural Match or a Compatible Number to your own numbers. You should try to avoid picking a name where it ultimately adds up as a Challenge Number to you. When you are working on a comparison chart, you should break down *the name you go by today,* and the *whole birth certificate name of the baby.* Below is a number comparison chart for Leeza Gibbons and her baby Nathan Daniel Meadows that shows you exactly what I am talking about.

LEEZA AND NATHAN'S CHART

EXPLANATION OF NUMBERS	LEEZA'S	NATHAN'S	COMBINED
SOUL NUMBER What you feel inside. Not necessarily what people see.	8	2	Natural Match
PERSONALITY NUMBER A face you show the world.	1	1	Natural Match
POWER NAME NUMBER This number represents the strength of your name. It is the most important number in your name.	9	3	Natural Match
BIRTH DAY The way you appear to people.	8	3	Challenge
LIFE PATH The number that you need to fulfill in order to be happy. The most important number in your personal Numerology.	6	3	Natural Match
ATTITUDE NUMBER The first impression people have when talking to you.	2	4	Natural Match

Note: Refer to page 13 to learn how to do a chart breadown.

▪ LEEZA AND NATHAN ▪

When Leeza Gibbons was pregnant with her third child, I was asked to make an appearance on her talk show. This particular episode was called "The Baby

Shower Show," and I was going to help Leeza pick out her baby's name using Numerology as a guide. Leeza knew she was going to have a boy and gave me three names that she and her husband, Steve, had picked out. To the first name, I responded that the child would have no problem spending her money. He would always want quality stuff and be very insistent on whatever his per-ceived needs were. The name numbers would also be a Challenge to Leeza's name numbers, and that would be a drain on her as a person, as well as her pocketbook! The second name choice would mean a very high-energy child, which would seek constant stimulation. As hectic as Leeza's schedule already was, this particular name number combination might be a little overwhelming for her.

Leeza then presented me with the name Nathan Daniel Meadows. I was completely taken by the beauty of the name, and I discovered it was an exel-lent match to Leeza's name numbers! Now that's what you hope for when you pick the name of a child.

I explained that all three numbers in the baby's name were Naturally Matched to her—very good news! I also showed that the child would have a 1-2-3 in his chart. What that means is if the child lives on the positive side of these numbers, then his life could be easy as 1, 2, 3. The 1 is for his ambition, the 2 for his capacity to love, and the 3 for his ability to be a charismatic com-municator. Leeza got the biggest kick out of this description. Well, the next time I spoke with her was at her real baby shower. I told her at the party that if the baby were born on a day breaking down to a 3 Life Path, it would be an ideal match to Leeza's 6 Life Path since the numbers 3 and 6 were Naturally Matched. She laughed and said she'd keep it in mind.

About a month later, Leeza went into the hospital and was in labor for well over 30 hours. Nathan was finally delivered by C-section on October 3, 1997—not only was the baby born on a 3 Birth Day, but was also a 3 Life Path!

Over the years, I've had occasion to speak with Leeza for various reasons and many times she has told me: "You know, Glynis, everything you said about what Nathan's personality would be is exactly what has come to pass." That's what is so powerful about naming a child by the numbers—you really can have a positive influence in helping to form the child's personality.

What this knowledge does is encourage you to promote peace and understanding with your child. It is all a mother could hope for. It's still going to be work, and you will undoubtedly have some challenges with your child. But thanks to the awareness of Numerology, Leeza has only one Challenge Number with Nathan. As I have explained throughout this book, if you only have one or two Challenge Numbers, there is nothing you cannot overcome. You'll butt heads occasionally, but overall there is peace and joy.

Leeza happens to be a 6 Life Path, which is the mother number, and this tells me that being a mom is extremely important to her. In spite of her demanding career, she has still managed to give birth to three children. She has this good heart, which comes from her 2 Attitude. She is known for her sensitivity, which is also why she makes such a great talk show host. But no matter how hard she works in her career, the numbers show that family is her top priority.

My forecast for Nathan is that he will somehow be involved in entertainment—maybe he'll wind up in front of the camera, doing a talk show, acting, or performing. With all those 3s in his chart, he is a natural. He has tremendous charisma from his birth numbers. This is definitely a child who will have all eyes on him. Nathan could also go into standup comedy, because 3s make the best comedians. I'm sure that his wit is already strong. No matter what the future has in store for Nathan, he and Leeza are both very lucky to be mother and son, with so many Natural Match Numbers in their charts. When you compare your chart, you will usually find a couple of Compatible Numbers, a couple of Challenge Numbers and one or two Natural Match Numbers. Leeza and Nathan have an amazing five Natural Matches. That is like hitting the Numerology jackpot! This Numerology connection testifies to a bond that is strong and somewhat magical.

▪ CHOOSING THE RIGHT NAME FOR YOUR CHILD ▪

Let's say you and your husband share a 2 in your charts. You would want your baby to have a 2 Destiny Number (the most important number that comes from the birth certificate name), since the 2 represents peacefulness and love. If you all have a 6, on the other hand, you might want to complement that by giving your child a 3 Destiny Number—which is a number that will bring more humor into the house. You can also take care to avoid numbers that are likely to cause conflict. If I had a 1 in my chart, I know that a fellow number 1 might want to compete with me. If I had an 8, I wouldn't want another 8 in the baby's name because I would want things to be easygoing, and 8s can feel Toxic to each other. If I wanted a high-energy child I'd pick a name that would add up to a 5. Refer back to chapter 7 for a more complete description of each Destiny Number, and the traits they represent.

I have a client who has an incredible bond with his nephew because they have four numbers out of five in common. The mother feels a bit jealous of the relationship, but the mother and her son share only one number, the number 9. Meanwhile, the uncle and child, with four out of five numbers, are of like mind, and they have a terrific time together. It was by explaining this to the mother that she began to feel less threatened by the uncle's relationship with her son.

If you don't have three numbers out of five with your baby, don't let that upset you. Just study all of the baby's vibrations and find out ways to encourage the child to live on the positive side of their numbers. At the end of this book I recommend, under suggested reading, books that will help you communicate better and get more of what you want from your children and family.

▪ NAMING YOUR PET ▪

I was once talking to a client who decided to play a trick on me. She asked me to describe the personality of someone close to her, based on the birthday and the name. I thought we were talking about a child, so I discussed its obstinate nature, its need for material possessions, and its finicky disposition. I had said the child was stuck up and did whatever he wanted, when he wanted. Suddenly my client was laughing until she cried—it turns out she had asked me to read her horse! And everything I'd said was true. My response was, "You've got to be kidding," but she went on to say that the horse was finicky and bolts out of the stable whenever it feels like it, and refuses to get going at the beginning of a ride. Even I was shocked—the accuracy in the breakdown was the same as if the horse had been a human. (By the way, the owner of the horse was a 6 Life Path. Remember what I said about a 6—if they don't have children, ask them about their pets and they will beam like proud parents!)

The lesson is that the personality of your pet can be influenced by what you call it. When you name your pets, you're giving them characteristics from those names. They take on that energy.

One of my clients had a dog named Poochie. I did the numbers of the dog's name, and it broke down to 8-9-8. I said that 8s like quality and go for the name brand, and she just laughed. She said, "Whenever I buy a cheaper brand of dog food, Poochie knocks the bowl right over and refuses to eat." He also decided his doghouse was getting shabby, and refused to sleep in it until she fixed it up.

People feel very connected to their pets—it's because of the unconditional love they give us. I believe it's also through the energy of their name as well as their date of birth. You usually can't pick the day of birth, but you can pick a name that is Naturally Matched, or Compatible to your Life Path Number. If you have a pet that is making you unhappy, a name change can make a big difference.

Let's look at some examples: Would you believe that TV icons Lassie and Barney are both 6-5-2s? The 6 in the Soul means parental, taking care of other people, the need to mother or father. You know Barney does it and Lassie did it as well. Appearing as the 5, which is freedom and adventure—gotta go, gotta do—the 5 energy means excitement. There was never a dull moment in either one of their character's lives. I'll tell you what's funny about the 5s—they are considered the entertainer, and as we go through all these other pet names, you're going to find a 5 in every one of them. If you have a pet you think is a ham, check out their numbers and see if there's a 5.

Everybody loved Lassie in her day, just as children today love Barney. I think it's interesting they have exactly the same numbers. The names Barney and Lassie add up to a 2, and 2s want love—wasn't Lassie hugged and kissed in every episode? Barney wants a hug all the time. When Barney walks in a room, the kids go crazy with excitement. His theme song is, "I love you, you love me. We're a happy family." Well, who better than a 2 to deliver that message?

Flipper is another TV pet that cracks me up. He's a 5-5-1, a double 5. A 5 in the soul means high energy. It is hard to catch up with a 5. A 5 will be in constant motion. What better description of a dolphin? Flipper lived in the ocean and never lacked for unexplored territory. His name added up to a 1, which is independent, self-motivated. Flipper was always trying to help people on land, even though he couldn't get on land to help them. This dolphin had charisma, and the double 5 energy would encourage that characteristic.

Let's look at a few more. Mr. Ed, Benji, and Felix (the cat) are all 4s. The 4 is knowledge, teaching us what we need to know.

What was Mr. Ed doing? He was always educating us. The 4 is the master of the mind, so A plus B must equal C. If you think back to Mr. Ed saying to his owner, "Oh, Wilbur!" implying that Wilbur didn't know as much as he did.

Whenever Felix had something to fix, he could reach into his "bag of tricks." A 4 vibration would definitely have a bag of tricks because they are the Mr. Fix-Its of this world. They can tackle any problem. Felix was very cerebral.

Let's take a look at Benji. If the robbers were after him, or any time there was trouble, he outsmarted everybody. He was constantly using his mind.

On a more personal note, I once had a beautiful cat named Jade—a 6-5-2. Just like Lassie and Barney, this cat was loaded with love. We tried to make her a house cat but could not because she had such a love of the outdoors. She just wanted to go out there and explore. One night she went out and disappeared. When we found her, she was badly wounded. There was no way to help her, so she had to be put to sleep. Anyone who owns a pet knows how devastating that was for me. I loved that cat.

Then I went looking for a new cat, and found one in an animal shelter. I had to think of a name for my new cat. I wanted a cat that liked to stay home and needed love. I named him Boe, which is a 2-2-4. The 2-2-4 needs love, lots of affection, and has a need for security. Boe does indeed give me lots of love and affection. Boe has a purr you would not believe. You touch this cat, his purr is so beautiful, you can hear it throughout the house.

One day Boe got out. What was so interesting was that when I came home, Boe had not left the porch steps. I could tell from the expression on his face that he was horrified to be outside. Boe was not remotely comfortable leaving his regular environment. Thinking back, Jade had the 5 vibration as her Personality Number, and she could not wait to find ways to get out of the house.

On that note, I go back to Felix, Benji, and Mr. Ed each having a 4 vibration. They all had a home. Mr. Ed felt safe in his stable. Benji had his home with the family, and Felix had his special house where he kept his magical bag of tricks.

If you look at your animals and break down the numbers, you're going to see exactly what I am talking about. Numerology is a science, and no matter what you break down, whether it's a pet, a baby, or a romantic interest, you're going to always see numerical patterns that come up again and again in your life. Since the Power Name Number represents the strength of the name, I have listed pet names under their Power Name Number. I also suggest that once you pick the pet's name you break it all the way down to look at the Soul Number and the Personality Number as well.

▪ PET POWER NAME DESCRIPTIONS AND SAMPLES ▪

Pet Power Name 1: Independent and loves to do what they want. If you are one who likes to show your pet, this is the vibration that would do well in competition. They will be very protective of the family and will intuitively know if something is wrong. Excellent Power Name Number for a watchdog.

Bono, Coconut, Bubba, Jelly, Roxy, Jinxy, Chewy, Chips, Chuck, Chunky, Copper, Frankie, Aloha, Amadeus, Anton, Bazel, Bobby, Fuji, Flash, Jewel, Joey, Butterscotch, Leon, Mina, Whiskey, Sissy, Crosby, Lancelot, Woody, Milla.

Pet Power Name 2: Loving, affectionate, and very loyal. This animal can really become your best friend. This pet will also instinctively know when you are unhappy, and want to comfort you.

Max, Buddy, Sassy, Caesar, Candy, Charlie, Jade, Cody, Yappy, Comet, Cougar, Donut, Cosmo, Ozzy, Cappuccino, Chopin, Nemo, Yogi, Watson, Sadie, Tilo, Winnie, Aristotle, Nugget, Chandler, Forrest, Kirby, Prince, Cinnamon.

Pet Power Name 3: They like to be close with their owners. They tend to be amusing and you will laugh at their antics. They know just what to do to get your attention.

Patch, Amos, Dag, Sasha, Zac, Ella, Lulu, Pickles, Sasha, Martini, Tai, Liza, Xina, Allie, Suzi, Jemmy, Lace, Rey, Yin, Uri, Jasmin, Duncan, Bree, Tyson, Pagan, Pluto, Ellis, Gard, Angel, Maxine.

Pet Power Name 4: These animals want to feel safe. Their home is very important to them and they are protective of it and you.

Kitty, Princess, Buster, Whiskers, Blue, Budd, Lola, Chewbacca, Coca, Cisco, Cookie, Daddles, Daisy, Dexter, Barnard, Farley, Fraser, Honey, Percy, Pepper, Sox, Chardonnay, Sushi, Alvin, Elvis, Kiki, Queenie, Trixie, Velvet, Star.

Pet Power Name 5: They want a lot of freedom to explore and are hard to control. A very playful energy and always ready for a walk or a game.

Bebe, Gigi, Whoopi, Tramp, Shasta, Bandit, Leo, Mango, Champ, Cherry, Choo, Dash, Bella, Aldo, Bessie, Tippy, Dolly, Edie, Walden, Jelly Bean, Bing, Blossom, Dewi, Duke, Voodoo, Misty, Tiger, Kippy, Lion, Waddles.

Pet Power Name 6: This animal is caring and protective, wants to be in charge of the home, and definitely acts like an important member of the family.

Tilly, Lady, Dino, Chester, Coolio, Cricket, Bangles, Dixie, Millie, Apple, Ruffles, Winston, Fanny, Ginger, Jasper, Lili, Pepe, Peach, Rio, Shorty, Scarlet, Skye, Spike, Topaz, Tulip, Tudor, Chester, Clinton, Peggy, Wilbur.

Pet Power Name 7: This will usually be a peaceful and loving animal who needs a lot of space and can sometimes have mood swings.

Pebbles, Chance, Chancie, Lucy, Amore, Chubby, Chops, Coors, Crankie, Basil, Ellie, Jiggs, Lester, Weenie, Clifton, Connor, Kasper, Kipp, Merry, Nixie, Poppy, Ryder, Tails, Burt, Dru, Yale, Otto, Dibble, Fitz, Hazel.

Pet Power Name 8: This pet wants the best that you have to offer. They enjoy the best food, a comfortable place to sleep, and often are, in some way, an exceptional-looking animal.

Oreo, Casper, Caramel, Boots, Chilli, Cosmic, Desert, Dante, Dobie, Dusty, Snow, Titus, Zeus, Milly, Mimi, Nili, Polly, Bongo, Gobbles, Roxie, Skipp, Ross, Crystal, Dewey, Elmer, Jasmine, Stinky, Smoochy, Scarlett.

Pet Power Name 9: This pet will be very loving and protective of the family. It is better to bring this pet on trips with you than to leave it behind. The 9 does not like to be left alone. If you cannot take the pet with you, then I suggest you have more than one pet so there is always companionship.

Lucky, Bambi, Butch, Bubbles, Cheerio, Bud, Chip, Coco, Cliff, Congo, Bagel, Buttercup, Dibbs, Fox, Red, Shamus, Tully, Kahlua, Bowie, Chilla, Shakespeare, Hattie, Vegas, Paris, Rocky, Pokey, Pixie.

▪ NAMING YOUR BUSINESS ▪

If I went into business for myself (as in my case a 3 Life Path), I would want to make sure that the business name was either Naturally Matched or Compatible with my Life Path Number. My business name is:

$$7+3+7+5+9+1 \quad 8+1+1 \quad 7+6+3+9 \quad 5+3+4+2+5+9=95$$

G l y n i s   H a s   Y o u r   N u m b e r

$$= 9+5 = 14 = 1+4 = 5$$

Which breaks down to a 5, and is a Compatible Number to my 3 Life Path. The 5 is also the sleuth. I'm constantly researching and digging into people's lives to find the numerical patterns.

In the case of a business name, break it down, and if that number is a Challenge Number to your Life Path Number, *don't use it*. You are setting yourself up to fail. If you are looking for a job, check the number of the company and make sure that it breaks down to either a Natural Match Number or a Compatible Number to your Life Path. If there's a choice of three jobs, pick the one that's most compatible to you in numbers. Numbers make it a lot easier to make a decision. Refer to chapter 3 to review how your Life Path gets along with each number.

When you are in the process of breaking down a company name, just use the name by which it is called—eliminate suffixes like Inc. or Ltd. (unless they are an intrinsic part of the name).

▪ NAMING YOUR CREATIVE PROJECT ▪

When you name something that you consider "your baby," such as a book, movie, or a business, you'll want the name to be Naturally Matched or Compatible to your Life Path. When you promote a venture, or pick specific dates to discuss it, it should again be on a day that is Naturally Matched or Compatible to your Life Path Number.

Let's look at an example that really shows the power of the numbers: Mel Gibson's movie *The Passion of the Christ*. This blockbuster triumph validates the science of Numerology. The title *The Passion of the Christ* breaks down to a 5, which is Naturally Matched to Mel's Life Path 7. When I talk to a client I would tell them that they should always pick a title that is Naturally Matched or Compatible to their Life Path number, thereby ensuring their own personal victory.

Moreover, when I read about Mel Gibson in *Entertainment Weekly*, I began to see a pattern. Mel Gibson is a 7 Life Path. I noticed that the date of the article was February 16 (1 + 6 = 7). The first big press release he did was February 7 (a 7 day), his interview with Diane Sawyer aired on television on February 16 (1 + 6 = 7). *Newsweek* did a story and the date on the cover was February 16, again a 7; February 25 is the day Mel Gibson released the movie (2 + 5 = 7). He also spent 25 million dollars on the movie (2 + 5 = 7). It would seem that Mel Gibson, perhaps intuitively, is applying basic Numerology.

I think it is also important to note that the number 7 is considered a very spiritual number. Some people refer to it as "God's favorite number." Looking just at Christianity, you can see that the number 7 has quite a role to play. Consider these Biblical teachings:

- The number 7 is used over 700 times in the Bible.
- In the Book of Revelations, the number 7 is used 54 times. There are 7 churches, 7 Spirits, 7 stars, 7 seals, 7 trumpets, 7 vials, 7 personages, 7 dooms, and 7 new things. God orchestrated a 7-year famine that followed on the heels of 7 good years.
- God created all things in the beginning and then took 6 days of restoring His creation and then rested on the 7th day (Genesis 2:1–3).

- Solomon was 7 years in building the Temple and kept the Feast for 7 days.
- Job had 7 sons. When his friends came to visit him they sat 7 days and 7 nights in silence, and afterward they were required to offer a burnt offering of 7 bullocks and 7 rams.
- There were 7 years of plenty and 7 years of famine in Egypt during the days of Joseph.

There is no disputing the fact that the number 7 is very significant when it comes to religious studies. A person with a 7 Life Path is here to find faith. Mel Gibson has certainly done that. He has been quoted as saying that the Holy Spirit worked through him, and he was just the vehicle when making the movie.

I have observed that the Life Path Number of a person will follow them around (see chapter 10 for more on this phenomenon), and this seems to be the case with Mel Gibson. They say that Mel Gibson's movie is the 7th best 3-day opening ever; it was also noted the movie averaged approximately $25,000 per theater.

There was a lot of speculation that the movie would fail because of the controversial subject matter. People also thought it would not succeed because the actors spoke in the dead languages of Aramaic and Latin. Yet, none of this interfered with the success of the movie. I believe it is because Mel Gibson is working in his Life Path of 7, which means he was coming from a sincere place and, for him, a place of truth.

Sixteen

Location, Location, Location:
Choosing Where to Live and Travel by the Numbers

For years now people have asked me, "Well, does it matter where I live? Does that make a difference in Numerology?" The answer is yes. It's important to know your location's vibration: The "location" includes the city, state, and country that you live in. I look at Numerology as an onion, because like life itself, when you peel it, you will find it has many layers. So the state, or country, is the outer layer of the onion, but you also need to peel it down into a city.

Consider the relationship between state and city to be the same as the numbers of your home address (state) and your apartment number (city). You might live at 7000 (7 + 0 + 0 + 0 = 7) Oak Street, apartment 2. Maybe the 7 of the street address isn't good for you, but the apartment number 2 is. The apartment number is the number whose vibration comes into your space.

This is the same with your city. Let's say you move to a state that's not a great match for you. The city—like the apartment—is the space in which you actually *live*. It will have a greater influence. Fortunately, you have more cities to choose from than states, so you have a good chance of finding one that is Compatible.

My client Barbara had to make a move to California, a state that breaks down to a 7. Barbara is a 3 Life Path, so this was a Challenge Number for her. Barbara was moving from New York, which is a 3 state—a Natural Match for her. Fortunately she was able to move to Hollywood, which breaks down to a 3 city. Almost immediately after arriving, she landed a great job as a sitcom writer. Since the city was Naturally Matched to her Life Path 3, it was no accident that things moved so smoothly for her. Had she moved into a city that was one of her Challenge Numbers (4, 7, 8), I'm sure the transition would have been much more difficult.

By the way, doesn't it make perfect sense that Hollywood, a center of creative activity, breaks down into a 3—the number of creative expression?

Sometimes you will feel called upon to go to a place. Intuitively you feel a bond with an area. For myself, I've always had a desire to go to Greece. This is a bit odd, because to tell you the truth, I'm not much of a traveler. But there it is. In my case, I had always thought it was because that's where Pythagoras was born, and Greece could be the site of a sacred spiritual experience for me. My studies in Numerology confirmed my intuitive feelings. Greece breaks down to the number 7, which is considered a spiritual vibration.

Nevertheless, Greece breaks down to a Challenge Number for me. So while it's fine for a visit, it's not the place I'm destined to live. I would never consciously live in a place that is a Challenge Number to my Life Path.

Now it's your turn. Do you have a country, state, or city in mind? Refresh yourself on the Natural Match and Compatible numbers for your Life Path (chapter 3) and then check the list below to see if your dream country, state, or city is good for you. What if your pick isn't on my list? Go ahead and break it down for yourself, by adding up the values of each letter from the Pythagorean chart on page 11. Here's an example:

$$7 + 9 + 5 + 5 + 3 + 5 = 34 = 3 + 4 = 7$$

G   R   E   E   C   E

Greece breaks down to a 7 vibration.

▪ COUNTRIES, STATES, AND CITIES BY THE NUMBERS: ▪

Vibration 1 Locations

- **Countries:** Antigua, Chile, Egypt, El Salvador, India, Israel, Morocco, Pakistan, Turkey, Vatican City
- **States:** Connecticut, District of Columbia, Idaho, Michigan, North Dakota, Rhode Island
- **Cities:** Chicago, Los Angeles, Louisville, Miami Beach, Milwaukee, Minneapolis, Portland, Seattle, Washington, DC

Vibration 2 Locations

- **Countries:** Ethiopia, France, Germany, Jamaica, Portugal, United Kingdom
- **States:** Colorado, Florida, Kansas, Kentucky, Louisiana, Minnesota, Nevada, Ohio, Oregon, Washington, DC
- **Cities:** Annapolis, Atlantic City, Fargo, Great Falls, Honolulu, Memphis, New Haven, Philadelphia, Seal Beach, Sydney

Vibration 3 Locations

- **Countries:** Australia, Cambodia, Denmark, Iceland, Venezuela, Vietnam
- **States:** Arizona, Arkansas, Iowa, Netherlands, New Mexico, New York, South Carolina, West Virginia
- **Cities:** Austin, Charlotte, Eugene, Grand Rapids, Hollywood, Nashville, Providence, Richmond, Salt Lake City, Santa Fe

Vibration 4 Locations

- **Countries:** Hungary, Italy, Kuwait, South Africa, United States, Virgin Islands
- **States:** Alabama, Mississippi, New Hampshire, North Carolina, Oklahoma, Washington
- **Cities:** Athens, Birmingham, Boston, Dallas, Des Moines, Houston, Jersey City, Madrid, Milan, Tallahassee

Vibration 5 Locations

- **Countries:** Angola, Belize, Brazil, Puerto Rico, Saudi Arabia, Spain, Taiwan
- **State:** Utah: Interestingly, the only one!
- **Cities:** Albuquerque, Baltimore, Boise, Chicago, Colorado Springs, Las Vegas, Pensacola, San Francisco, Sun Valley, Tokyo

Vibration 6 Locations

- **Countries:** Belgium, Canada, Delaware, Finland, Guam, Iran, Japan, Mexico, New Zealand, Norway, Palau, Peru, Russia
- **States:** Maine, Massachusetts, Missouri, Montana, Texas
- **Cities:** Atlanta, Bridgeport, Cincinnati, Flagstaff, Indianapolis, New York City, Raleigh, Rome, Tampa, Yuma

Vibration 7 Locations

- **Countries:** Armenia, Bolivia, Colombia, Fiji, Greece, Monaco, Sweden, Switzerland
- **States:** California, Indiana, Maryland, New Jersey, Tennessee, Wyoming
- **Cities:** Bangkok, Charleston, Cheyenne, Corpus Christi, Jacksonville, Orlando, Pasadena, Reno, St. Louis, Tacoma

Vibration 8 Locations

- **Countries:** Algeria, Andorra, Argentina, Austria, Barbados, China, Costa Rica
- **States:** Georgia, Nebraska, Pennsylvania, Vermont, Virginia, Wisconsin
- **Cities:** Cedar Rapids, Fort Collins, Little Rock, Maui, Montreal, Ojai, Santa Barbara, Tallahassee, Vail, Yosemite Valley

Vibration 9 Locations

- **Countries:** Bahamas, Cuba, Guatemala, Iraq, Zimbabwe
- **States:** Alaska, Illinois, South Dakota
- **Cities:** Buffalo, Geneva, Hartford, Helena, Mexico City, Miami, New Orleans, Paris, Spokane, Toronto

▪ WHEN YOUR DREAM VACATION IS A CHALLENGE NUMBER: LOCATION VIBRATION DESCRIPTIONS ▪

What if you are going on a trip and you discover that your destination breaks down to a number that is a Challenge Number to your Life Path? Then you need to focus on the positive side of the location's energy. Remember that even though the locale may vibrate with a Challenge Number, each and every number is positive in its own right. Here's a brief summary of what to expect from each vibration location.

1 Vibration Location Summary: This is a good place to establish your independence and feel like you are in charge. Watch out for being hypercritical.

2 Vibration Location Summary: This is a good place to get in touch with your inner peace and possibly find love. Watch out for being oversensitive.

3 Vibration Location Summary: This is a good place for laughter and communication. Watch out for talking too much and saying something you will regret later. Be open to listening to what others have to say.

4 Vibration Location Summary: This is a good place to educate yourself and gain knowledge. Watch out for being too blunt when having a conversation. Try to be spontaneous.

5 Vibration Location Summary: This is a good place for beauty, adventure, and excitement. Watch out for overindulgence.

6 Vibration Location Summary: This is a good place to feel nurtured and protected. Watch out for seeming too in control, let your needs be known.

7 Vibration Location Summary: This is a good place to spend time alone and get in touch with your inner voice. Watch out for being too antisocial—you will be able to find real wisdom in other people.

8 Vibration Location Summary: This is a good place for the aesthetic beauty of the location and possibly to work. Watch out for overreacting to trivial problems. Trust that everything will fall into place.

9 Vibration Location Summary: This is a good place for a humanitarian pursuit and to evolve as a human being. Watch out for feeling lost or confused. Don't be afraid to ask for help.

▪ YOUR HOME ADDRESS ▪

My own house number adds up to a 7, which is a cerebral number with a vibration that encourages solitary thought. Since my office is also in my home, I strive to create an atmosphere that encourages teamwork. That's why I took a 3 and a 1 and placed them on the inside of my door. This turned my 7 house into a 2 energy ($7 + 1 + 3 = 11 = 1 + 1 = 2$). I found that with each employee there was peace and understanding whenever I gave instructions.

But recently, my home environment radically shifted. Where once there had been a collegial atmosphere, I suddenly found my employees fighting over petty things. There was an air of defiance here, and I was completely mystified. As soon as I realized what was going on, I went to check my door. Lo and behold, the 1 had fallen off the door—I was now suddenly living in a 1-vibration house! The 1 vibration encourages competitiveness and the need to win. This is why simple conversations had turned into debates, and why we were all suddenly at odds on every single issue.

I immediately put the 1 back on the door, returning the house energy to the calming influence of the 2, and the effect was instantaneous. Although the peo-

ple who work for me continue to be strong-minded, we are once again respect-
ful of one another.

The house number makes all the difference in the world. So how do you
break down an address? The actual number is the most important. If you live in
an apartment, it's the number on your door.

If you live in a house that's 1000 Maple Drive, it's the 1 that's important
because $1 + 0 + 0 + 0 = 1$. If you live in an apartment and the apartment number is 320-B, break 320 ($3 + 2 + 0 = 5$) down to a 5 and break down the B using the Pythagorean chart (see p. 11), and add it to the number 5. According to
the Pythagorean Chart, B is a 2, so $5 + 2 = 7$. That is the vibration coming into
that apartment. If you live in a rural area where there are no numbers involved,
but just a street name, then break down the street name.

Let's look closely at these examples: You live at 1000 Park Street, apartment 8. The 1000 breaks down to a 1, so that's the energy of the complex you
live in—in this case it's ambition, determination, being the best at what you do.
The apartment number has an even bigger impact on what's going on inside the
apartment. In this example it's an 8, so the energy encourages you to strive for
financial freedom, and to do things that make a difference on a grand scale.
This is an address that would support executive success and promote ambition.

Say you live on Oak Street, and yours is the only house, so there is no number. You would simply use the Pythagorean system and break down all the letters (consonants and vowels) to

6+1+2 1+2+9+5+5+2 = 33
| | | | | | | | |
O A K   S T R E E T

$3 + 3 = 6$

This becomes a 6 home, which represents family. It's a good house to
choose if you already have a family, or if you are hoping to have one. It's also
ideal to live in if you are searching for a warm and safe environment.

Below you'll find a summary and then longer descriptions of the different houses you may live in, 1 through 9. Refer back to these definitions when you're searching for a new home or if you would like to change the energy in your house to something more appropriate for your life. Note that the term "house" applies to apartments as well.

▪ A SUMMARY OF HOUSE ENERGIES ▪

The 1 house is a place to establish independence.

The 2 house is a house of love and partnership.

The 3 house is a house of laughter and communication.

The 4 house is a house of security and a place of safety.

The 5 house is a great house for parties, entertainment, and drama.

The 6 house is a house of beauty and warmth, and a magnet for children.

The 7 house is a house of study and intellectual development.

The 8 house is a house that encourages financial achievement.

The 9 house is a house of the extrovert—all are welcome.

The 1 House: A 1-vibration home means you would be motivated. Let's say you're living somewhere now where you feel none of your dreams are happening. Well, then it would be time to move into a 1 home, because that means you become the best at what you do and you forge ahead. You don't necessarily need help; you have a vision and you achieve it. You feel very confident in your choices. When you live in a 1 home, you can achieve excellence. This is not necessarily a home to be involved with someone else. Let's say you've been in a bad marriage and you want to move and take care of yourself and establish independence because you've been too dependent on others.

The 1 home would be ideal for that reason. If you are looking for love, you would not necessarily want to move into a 1 home, because that wouldn't encourage a partnership.

The 2 House: The 2 home encourages love. So let's say you're about to get married. To ensure that the relationship would be stable and long-lasting, it wouldn't hurt to move into a 2 home, because the energy of the home is encouraging love, harmony, and partnership. It's also the kind of home that seeks peace; there wouldn't be much conflict because the home wouldn't embrace it.

Let's say someone came in upset. In no time flat they'd start to feel better because the home would have a natural beauty and peace that says: "It's okay to just relax." You should have music, candles, plants, flowers, and all of nature's beauty here in the home of 2. This is a place to tap into your psychic ability and trust your inner voice, because in a 2 home you'll find more spirituality than usual. The 2 house nurtures relationships.

The other thing about a 2 home, it's the kind of home where you can never have enough. If you have a party there, there's always more than enough food or more than enough people because there's such a need to make everyone feel welcome. The down side of a 2 home is you have to be careful not to be too enmeshed in your partner's problems. If they do come home in pain, you have to be careful not to jump in and fall into the pain with them. You need to be able to step back and say, "I'm sorry that happened, but let's work on it together." Listen with empathy, but be able to step back. I would caution the couple that the relationship can be so all-encompassing that other people don't feel welcome; they feel they are intruding on your little safe harbor. We are on a planet with millions of other people and you have to bring others in to let them have a taste of that lovely peace you have found in your 2 home.

The 3 House: The 3 house is all about communication and self-expression. There should be plenty of laughter here and enjoyment of the people in it. Everyone can come here, no matter how eccentric, and feel welcome in this home. This is a home of celebration, of unconditional love, of saying: "Whoever you are, it's okay." It's a great place to have parties and entertain. You also will find there's passion here.

You have to be careful about money, because as is typical of 3 energy, 3s are having so much fun they think, Play now, pay later, and the next thing you know you're in debt and you're in trouble. So you've got be careful about that scattered energy. In the house of 3 you can find you have so much energy you feel you can do anything, and you should use this affirmation daily: "From the ocean of abundance, money always comes to me." Repeat fifteen to twenty minutes a day, so that money is not an issue.

The 4 House: The 4 home represents security. Let's say you're living somewhere right now where you're very insecure. You feel like nothing has come together, and you're not safe. Move into the 4 home because there's a sense of peace and a feeling of *I'm okay*. The 4 house is grounded; it's all about the earth. There should be a garden or flowers in the backyard. Definitely have plants in this home. The 4 home is solid, and there is a great foundation, which makes people feel protected.

It's a home to seek knowledge and become better at whatever it is you've chosen in your career. The 4 is also a house of service, so if you work for a charitable organization, you should meet in a 4 home. As a matter of fact, there's a Girl Scout house in my neighborhood that has a 4 address. The girls are really making a difference. They are giving to charities and making a lot of people happy. The 4 home is all about that. There will be a feeling of constantly working. If you are going to college and have to study a lot, the house of 4 would be an ideal location, but please remember to enjoy yourself from time to time. You really have to be silly once in a while, so find ways to keep yourself amused. If you don't loosen up in a 4 house, it can become too intense.

The 5 House: If you live in a 5 house, it's just nonstop. It's vibrant, alive. The people in this house are involved in all kinds of activity. This can be with the town itself, going to meetings, getting involved in charities. If it's children, it can be extracurricular activities, sports, drill team, cheerleading, etc. The house of 5 is about celebrating holidays, and a place to party.

It has to be beautiful and enchanting. You definitely feel passionate and alive there. If anything, you need to be careful not to get involved in some type of scandal like an affair with a neighbor. If you are in a partnership, husband and wife, be sure to converse about your feelings so that your needs are being met in the relationship. The 5 house is going to make you aware of what is lacking. It is all about the five senses, and you will be keenly aware of your surroundings.

If you were depressed and had a friend who lived in a house of 5, you would definitely want to go over there to visit because you would immediately feel the excitement and energy of being alive. That's what the house of 5 exudes. Don't be too quick to make drastic decisions. If you're not happy in your marriage in the house of 5, don't break up immediately, because chances are you'll regret it later. It would be better to go to counseling and maybe even take a trip to get away, take an objective look, and then come back. Your instincts can ultimately be good in a house of 5, but don't move too fast. Be deliberate in your choices before you decide to do anything.

The 6 House: The house of 6 is a striking home and if you lived there as a husband and wife starting a family, this would be a terrific place to raise your children. This is also a place to effectively run your company out of your home: It could be counseling, aromatherapy, massage therapy, or anything to do with helping people feel better. When people walk into a house of 6, they feel taken care of. If I were to caution you in your 6 home, it would be, don't give so much that eventually you're exhausted and drained and feel no one's giving back. Also, when things are going well in the house of 6, don't think it's going so well that it's too good to be true. Be sure you embrace the peacefulness and harmony of the home. Since 6 energies tend to stay home, make sure you don't just go home to your refuge and stop having company. Definitely invite people in.

It's an ideal place to raise children, because they would feel taken care of and be willing to listen and learn from you. What we are all seeking is a place that we can call our home, and in the house of 6, we find that. Having acceptance for others is easy in the house of 6. There is an understanding of people. A perfect home for a counselor or advisor.

The 7 House: The house of 7 is a home where you should be contemplating life and looking deep inside yourself. The adventure is within. There will be a real need to start investigating and reading different books. Learning more about who you are and what you are doing. The 7 energy is the one that needs to find faith and I think in a house of 7 you are going to be tested on that level.

You have to be careful not to escape through sex, drugs, alcohol, or food. This is a time to just look inside yourself, also write (definitely keep a journal in the house of 7). This is a great place for a doctor, a scientist, or a student who has to become an expert in his field. This is also a place to study your dreams and visions. People may find they have more intuition than usual in a house of 7. Maybe they have dreams that come true or find that ghosts come into the home because they feel welcome there.

This is not a home for people who are seeking to advance materially. If you live in a 7 house or if you live in an apartment number 7 and feel, Gosh, that's not fair, you can always add a letter to that energy, such as putting an A on the inside of the door. A is 1, which would make it a house of 8, and that would help you on a financial level. I'm a firm believer that we can always alter the energy we are living in.

You do have a tendency to feel like a loner in the house of 7. The 7 energy encourages you to be alone with nature and your thoughts. If you are in a relationship, make an extra effort to communicate with your partner.

The 8 House: The 8 house represents abundance in all areas of your life. You can have many friends, make money, be materially prosperous, and come into your feeling of power; but while you are living in your house of 8, some people can perceive you as ruthless in the way you go about your business. You have to be careful what you're communicating to the people outside your 8 house because it can breed jealousy.

This is a powerful house. This is a home for a politician or anybody who is dealing with people and needs them to respect what they have to say. This is a home for people who have organizational or managerial skills. They can prosper and benefit in a house of 8.

This is also a house that is usually beautifully decorated or has a quality of elegance to it. If you have children, make sure the children feel appreciated. If you have a wife, take the time to send her cards and flowers, because otherwise there will be resentment. In the 8 home, the occupants can feel unloved by the breadwinner. So keep that in mind in the house of 8.

The 9 House: The house of 9 is the house of the humanitarian. If you live in a house of 9, people look to you for advice or counsel because it is a very evolved house. People who live in it should feel blessed and want to make a difference.

A house of 9 is a selfless vibration where you feel the need to give to others while living there. It puts you in touch with the universal truth. Understand that what you give is what you get back. It's a very charitable home to be in and people will always be drawn to you while living in a 9 home. You might also be visited by people from your past. If you were upset with your parents, this might be a time to write letters of forgiveness, to let it go, to tie up all these loose ends and clear things out.

This is not a house to have clutter, but a place where you need to make room for new things coming in. It's all about the abundance of the universe and trusting that the process is inevitably going to affect you in a great way. You are in touch with the Holy Spirit or your Higher Power, and as a result you can help change the world for the better in the house of 9. Chances are in this house you can see what's good in people, because we all have positive and negative sides. Kahlil Gibran says in *The Prophet*:

"Speak to me of the good and evil in people. I can speak only of the good. Not the evil. Evil is just a good person who has lost the way. If you're lost, you're going to eat from a dark cave, you're going to drink from dark water."

Simply meaning we're all human. We're all trying to find our way. In a house of 9, you may find yourself feeling concerned for the people who come into your life, but be careful not to let your energy get drained.

The 11 and 22 Houses: If you live a house that is the Master Number 11, know that this is a powerful house for intuition. This is good for anything to do with spiritual healing. (Remember that I said Master Numbers could heal people.) It's also about developing your excellence; picking your focus and achieving it.

The 22 house is about mental mastery. All this study and knowledge will come through you and then you've got to use it. If you are a writer and you write a book in this house, chances are the book will be published. In the house of 22, you will be perfecting your physical, emotional and mental health.

Note: See chapter 16 on creating different vibrations if you feel like your house number isn't right for you. But remember, no matter where you are moving or where you live, don't get upset and think, Gosh, I live in a house of 3 and I don't want to be here. Where you live right now is exactly where you belong *at this moment*. This is the lesson you are learning. When you are through with the lesson, you will instinctively know when it is time to move on.

Seventeen

Picking Other Important Numbers

There are so many numbers in our lives—some we get to choose, others are assigned to us. Either way, knowing what vibrations are coming from the numbers that surround you gives you an enormous amount of information to work from. Here are a few examples.

▪ PHONE NUMBERS ▪

Depending on where you live and the service in your area, you may or may not have a hand in choosing your phone number. But if you have the opportunity, be sure to choose one that brings in the influence that makes sense for you.

What number you should look for depends on the purpose of that phone in your life. For the sake of simplicity, let's assume you have a business in your home. If it's a computer business, try to get a number that breaks down to a 4 or 7. If you're a performer or entertainer, try for a 3 or 5. If your business is fiercely competitive, go for a number that breaks down to a 1. If your career is in caregiving—perhaps you're a nurse—try a number that adds up to a 2. If none of the above applies, you can always try for a 6. A 6 energy will make sure that business goes your way. Note that when you break down a phone number, you do not include the area code when picking the vibration.

For example: 497-2598 = 4 + 9 + 7 + 2 + 5 + 9 + 8 = 44 = 4 + 4 = 8

Here is a list of the basic definitions of 1 through 9 when you are looking for a phone number:

If It's a 1 Phone Number: It is for independent reasons. A person who is striving to be number one. A perfect phone number for someone who is in competitive sports, in charge of an important fund-raiser, or maybe someone who does top sales.

If It's a 2 Phone Number: It is for love, peace, and harmony. It could be a great number for a hospital or for your family's home, where you want nothing but love coming through the phone lines.

If It's a 3 Phone Number: It is for communication. A perfect number for a company that does high volume in sales or a cell phone where you want a lot of people to call.

If It's a 4 Phone Number: It is for a solid business. A phone number where there's knowledge: school or a library, etc.

If It's a 5 Phone Number: It is for having a good time. A number for constant stimulation with an exciting, busy atmosphere. It would be a great number for a party-planning company, a nightclub, or perhaps a travel agency.

If It's a 6 Phone Number: It is magnetic. This number would subconsciously command respect and would be ideal for the owner of a company.

If It's a 7 Phone Number: It is for privacy. Ideal for a detective agency, or a place where only authorized people have access to the phone number. Perfect for any private or emergency line.

If It's an 8 Phone Number: It is for big business such as betting lines at a racetrack, stock exchange, international business, or where the possibility of increasing your income is involved.

If It's a 9 Phone Number: It is for volunteer work or a business taking care of lots of people. The American Red Cross should use this number. It is also a great home phone number because it is all about family.

▪ HOTEL ROOMS ▪

Depending on why you're traveling, try to pick a number that's compatible with your goal. For example, if you're traveling for romance and excitement, you're looking for a 5. If it's love and harmony you seek, try for a 2. If you're on a business trip and want to have the competitive edge, go for a 1. If you're getting away for some quiet time to study or write, ask for a number that breaks down to a 4 or 7. The 8 is a good number for a money-related trip, while the 9 or 6 is the right energy if you're visiting family or attending a funeral. The 3—the number for humor and laughter—would be appropriate if you're throwing a party in the room, be it bachelor/bachelorette or birthday. It is important to remember that whatever the number is on the hotel room door needs to be reduced to one digit. Example: Hotel Room 562, $5 + 6 + 2 = 13 = 1 + 3 = 4$. Hotel Room 562 is a 4 room.

▪ LUCKY LOTTO NUMBERS ▪

The question I get asked all the time is, "What are my lucky numbers?" Everyone wants to know which are the best numbers for winning the lottery or any competition where numbers are involved. That's why I've created a list below of each Life Path's luckiest days, months, and best numbers.

But before we get there, I have some fascinating news for 5 Life Paths. Choosing lucky numbers is one of the hottest topics in my line of work, and I decided to do some research in Las Vegas. I found that out of 100 people I approached in a casino, 80 of those people had a 5 in their birth numbers. I then did a television segment called "Lucky Lotto Winners," where I researched the birth numbers of multiple-million-dollar winners to search for a pattern. Of the four I found, *all of them were a 5 Life Path*.

So all you 5s out there, the odds seem to be in your favor! But use your common sense—don't play with money you can't afford to lose, like money you need for rent or a car payment. If you're not a 5 Life Path and you want to play, try asking a 5 Life Path friend to bet for you.

▪ LUCKY NUMBERS BY LIFE PATH ▪

Lucky Stats for the Life Path 1
- Best months: January and October
- Best days of the month: 1, 10, 19, and 28
- Best day of the week: Sunday
- Lucky numbers: 1, 10, 19, 28, 37, 46, 55, 64, 73, 82, 91, and 100

Lucky Stats for the 2 Life Path
- Best months: February and November
- Best days of the month: 2, 11, 20, and 29
- Best day of the week: Tuesday
- Lucky numbers: 2, 11, 29, 38, 47, 56, 65, 74, 83, 92, and 101

Lucky Stats for the 3 Life Path
- Best months: March and December
- Best days of the month: 3, 12, 21, and 30
- Best day of the week: Wednesday
- Lucky numbers: 3, 12, 21, 39, 48, 57, 66, 75, 84, 93, and 102

Lucky Stats for the 4 Life Path
- Best month: April
- Best days of the month: 4, 13, 22, and 31
- Best day of the week: Thursday
- Lucky numbers: 4, 13, 22, 31, 40, 49, 58, 67, 76, 85, 94, and 103

Lucky Stats for the 5 Life Path
- Best month: May
- Best days of the month: 5, 14, and 23
- Best day of the week: Tuesday
- Lucky numbers: 5, 14, 23, 32, 41, 50, 59, 68, 77, 86, 95, and 104

Lucky Stats for the 6 Life Path
- Best month: June
- Best days of the month: 6, 15, 24
- Best days of the week: Sunday, Monday, and Friday
- Lucky numbers: 6, 15, 24, 33, 42, 51, 60, 69, 78, 87, 96, and 105

Lucky Stats for the 7 Life Path
- Best month: July
- Best days of the month: 16 and 25
- Best days of the week: Saturday you do well with people, Sunday you should be alone or with a kindred spirit
- Lucky numbers: 7, 16, 25, 34, 52, 61, 70, 79, 88, 97, and 106

Lucky Stats for the 8 Life Path
- Best month: August
- Best days of the month: 8, 17, and 26
- Best day of the week: Thursday
- Lucky numbers: 8, 17, 26, 35, 44, 53, 62, 71, 80, 89, 98, and 107

Lucky Stats for the 9 Life Path
- Best month: September
- Best days of the month: 9, 18, and 27
- Best days of the week: Monday alone, Friday with companions
- Lucky numbers: 9, 18, 27, 36, 45, 54, 63, 72, 81, 90, 99, and 108

Eighteen

When Numbers Follow Us Around

Through the years, people have written to me and talked about certain number patterns and wonder what they mean. They often say the numbers are following them around! It's true; once you realize how much power the numbers have, you'll start noticing certain numbers are always cropping up. I've noticed that when a 3 Life Path client needs me, they'll call me at 1:11, which adds up to a 3. A 7 Life Path will call me at 2:05, which is a 7. Tonight while typing this book, a good friend who is a 9 Life Path left a message on my answering machine at 9:54 P.M. Of course it was a 9 moment! Once you know the numbers, you'll begin to recognize that these patterns are already occurring in your life.

■ 11:11 ■

My favorite example of the reoccurring numbers is when people see 11:11 on the clock. When you see 11:11, what it means is that the universe has opened up to receive whatever it is that you want. I once read that the universe has one answer and that answer is "YES." So if you say, "I can do it. I can achieve the dream," the answer is, "Yes. You can do it. You can achieve the dream." But if you say, "I can't do it, it will never happen," then the answer is, "YES, you CAN'T do it and it will never happen." In the moment of 11:11, the universe is open to whatever it is that you want, so I literally will spend the whole minute saying things like, "I have financial security in my life. I can afford to buy the new home that I want. I bless the relationship that I'm in, and I affirm that it can only get better." You can say whatever it is that you want for that full minute, and it will have an impact on your life. I have many people write me and tell me what a difference it has made for them. A client named Greg wrote telling me that his girlfriend was breaking up with him, and that he didn't want it to end. He said each day he would watch for 11:11 in the morning and at night. He would then ask that as a couple, they find a way to compromise, and that she would realize that they belonged together. Sure enough, she came back to him one month later and now they are both working on the relationship. He said what astounded him is that she actually said the words "they really did belong together," exactly what he kept affirming when the clock hit 11:11. Greg gives full credit of this blessing in his life to the influence of 11:11. So next time you see 11:11, know that it is in fact a powerful moment and a chance to ask for what it is you truly want.

▪ NUMBERS IN A SEQUENCE ▪

Some people have said that they will see certain numbers in a particular sequence, such as 3, 3, 3. It could be on the numbers on the clock when they happen to look at it, or the price of some food they have just purchased. They always ask, "What the heck does it mean?" When a number repeats itself, I look at the individual number first to understand its meaning. The 3 represents communication. When I see 3, 3, 3 I say it is a message to you, encouraging you to speak up, or really say what it is that you are feeling. You may find that you are withholding your true feelings and the 3, 3, 3 is saying, "Tell us what you really think!" If you add all the numbers together (3 + 3 + 3), it becomes a 9. It may be a reminder about poor communication with your family or unresolved issues that you need to let go. When you look at the number, look at it for its actual essence from the basic definitions of 1 through 9, and then you will be able to come up with an answer that will make sense to you. If I see 2, 2, 2, it symbolizes love and serenity. Why? Because the number 2 is the number that represents love. If I break it down to one digit (2 + 2 + 2) it becomes a 6. This is reminding me to promote love, peace, and harmony in my family. If you see 4, 4, 4, I say this is a message about seeking more knowledge, doing what it takes to learn more and educate yourself. Why? Because the 4 is all about learning. If I break it down to one digit (4 + 4 + 4), it becomes a 3. That means I need to communicate to others whatever it is that I am learning. I should not keep it to myself. So always think of the basic definition of the one number that is repeating itself, then break the repeating number down to one digit, and it will give you a clear understanding of its significance.

▪ WHEN YOU SEE YOUR NATURAL MATCH NUMBERS ▪

The number pattern that I see all the time are my Natural Match Numbers, which are 3, 6, and 9. I usually see them on various license plates when I am driving around. I also see them on a price tag at the supermarket, or on the clock. Every time I see it, I feel that it is a special message just for me. Let's look at each number separately. 3 is laughter, playfulness; the 6 is the magnetic vibration, people are drawn to you; 9 is the highest number and kindhearted. This gives me a quick insight into what these numbers represent for me. When I see 3, 6, 9 it reminds me that I am on the right track, and that everything is going to be all right. So if you see your Natural Match Numbers, which could also be 1, 5, 7 or 2, 4, 8, think of it as a positive message to you from the universe.

▪ A SPECIAL EXAMPLE: 9/11 ▪

The other one that I see a lot and that I have clients tell me about is 9/11. I've seen 9/11 on the clock quite a bit, about four or five times a week, and I believe it's a message of *"You must never forget." Never forget* what we went through on 9/11/2001. It was a tragedy and it was a momentous event for all of us. The message being that you need to make the most of your day, because you don't know when it is your last day. It's about living and being grateful that you are still here to make a difference and to find ways to be happy. The poor victims of 9/11 lost their lives and did not see it coming. When I see 9/11, that is what the message means to me.

Nineteen

Special Numbers and Patterns

After studying Numerology for so many years, I've come to recognize some special attributes that attach themselves to particular numbers or patterns of numbers. I'd like to share these with you, just in case these same numbers and patterns appear in your chart or those of your loved ones. They provide additional insight and may help you better understand your own motivations! They are the 1-8-9 number pattern, the Life Path 7/Birth Day 3 combo, the A/J/S, the misunderstood 8, and the search for your missing numbers.

▪ THE 1-8-9 NUMBER PATTERN ▪

When I see a chart that contains the numbers 1, 8, and 9 as the name numbers, I know that this person has what it takes to be extremely successful. There are so many examples in the entertainment industry alone that I can't possibly list them all. So here's a sampling.

Dick Clark is a 1-8-9 and an ageless icon who began his career in television in 1945 working from the mailroom up. Early on in his career he proved to be a true humanitarian and businessman. He changed *Bandstand* to *American Bandstand*, ended the all-Caucasian policy, and began introducing African-American artists. In 1957 he formed Dick Clark Productions, which in 2002 sold for $140 million. His hectic schedule has not slowed down much at all. He continues to host *America's Top 40* and still does the New Year's Eve count-down in Times Square. While most of Dick Clark's contemporaries are happily retired, he continues to thrive.

Gwyneth Paltrow, another one whose name breaks down to a 1-8-9, is an Oscar-winning actress who picks and chooses her roles. The daughter of a fairly well-known actress and director, Gwyneth shot straight to the A-list and is now considered Hollywood royalty.

Brad Pitt is another 1-8-9. He's a member of the $20-million club, and women are crazy about him. The fact that he's married to one of the most beloved actresses in Hollywood doesn't seem to bother his fans or *People* magazine, who named him Sexiest Man Alive for the second time after he was wed.

Catherine Zeta-Jones is another 1-8-9. Not just an Oscar-winning actress, she holds lucrative contracts with T-Mobile and Red Door. You might say she has her own version of the $20-million club: That was the amount she received from Michael Douglas on their wedding day as part of the prenuptial agree-ment. The woman knows how to keep herself in the limelight.

And the list goes on!

So what does the 1-8-9 mean? Well, the 1 is the Soul Number. A 1 in the Soul means ambition, to strive to be the best you can be. The 8 is the Personal-ity Number. The 8 means you are business minded. When you think of show business, show is a part of it, but *business* is what it is all about. The 9 Power Name Number is the highest number in Numerology. It is a number we sub-consciously look up to and respect as the leader. It is no accident that so many people who are successful in show business where so many of us look for our role models have the 1-8-9 name numbers.

So if you are reading this and you have the name numbers 1-8-9 and you are wondering if you have what it takes to make it in show business, then I say, "Yes you do!" Why? Because it's in your numbers!

▪ BIRTH DAY 3, LIFE PATH 7 ▪

Another pattern I've found arises in people born on a 3 day with a 7 Life Path. These people confuse the heck out of those around them! When you're born on a 3 day you look like someone who's very approachable—someone who wants to talk openly and share his or her innermost thoughts. But when you're a 7 Life Path your need for privacy is sacred to you, and you don't want anyone prying into your personal life. So when people start asking questions of this "open and sharing" Birth Day 3, he or she starts to feel uncomfortable. The 7 Life Path jumps in and says, "Well, why are you asking me this? Why do you want to know that?" This combination is truly a case of "what you see is not what you get." If you have this combo in your chart, make sure you let people know up front how much you value your privacy. This will go a long way in preventing discord.

▪ THE A/J/S ▪

Another pattern I've discovered in my years of readings deals with letters, rather than numbers. I am referring to the letters A/J/S. I call it the A/J/S pattern, and it appears when there are two letters that break down to the 1-vibration energies within a name. If you look at the Pythagorean chart on page 11, you'll see that the letters that break down to the vibration 1 are A, J, and S. So, when any two of these letters are found in one name—names like Jason, Janice, Sally, Sam, James, or Sarah, for example—you'll see this pattern emerge. These double-1 people share two traits: They tend to be exceptionally talented; they don't realize how good they are. It's a lot of work to raise a child with that particular name because they require so much feedback, and then when they get older they can put you on an emotional roller coaster. Since the name adds up to a double 1, when they get upset or feel threatened, just like a 2 Life Path, they can become the terrible 2 and throw a tantrum.

A famous example would be Sally Field—SA. Sally won two Oscars and by the time she had won that second one, she said, "Oh, you like me, you really like me." What it took for her to realize we liked her! Needless to say, most actresses would be thrilled to even be nominated. It took her two wins to start to believe we cared about her because her own esteem was so damaged.

Then there's Jane Fonda, JA, with her physical fitness empire saying to the masses, "Just take your body and make it the best you can. Be the best you can be with what you've got." Next thing you know, she got breast implants, which completely invalidated what she was teaching. Her underlying message was: "No matter how good you are, you're still not good enough." And that's what I mean about a double 1 that is hurting.

Now, the affirmation I would give this double-1 energy would be to repeat ten to fifteen minutes a day, looking straight into their eyes in a mirror, "I recognize the miracle of my being. I am enough." At first their eyes will look back at them like they're nuts, "Boy, you are narcissistic, you think you're so great," but as they continue to do this, eventually there will be a warmth and love in their eyes; and because they are putting this out, people will be less competitive with them, and realize that they're actually coming from a good place. There is something about that double-1 energy that seems kind of smug and self-important, and I really believe it's because they do like to win; they like to be the best, and yet they never think they're that good. It's the ultimate paradox.

When Sally Field made that famous acceptance speech, "You like me—you really like me," people were offended. Was anyone more raked over the coals? And yet she was totally vulnerable when she said it. She was crying, she meant it, but that's not what they heard. I have the tape of her actually accepting her Oscar and crying. Very few people could identify with her sincere pain. They just thought, Who do you think you are? You win two Oscars and you want us to validate you! It was something society does not allow us to do, and yet it was a truly honest declaration for her. And later, she wound up doing a parody of herself, making fun at the next Oscar ceremony, saying, "You liked it, you really liked it."

What I would say to a mother who reads this and says, "That's my child's name," is know that you need to nurture that child, and be aware. Always address their positive before their negative. As I've said before, say to a child who's not getting homework done, but maybe their room looks terrific: "I'm really pleased with your room, I can't believe how you put everything away. So tonight, let's get to work on your homework, okay?" Because once they get that little bit of encouragement, it makes all the difference in the world and then they can build their confidence.

For you parents who read this and realize you have named your child a double-1 vibration name, just know that you need to be especially aware as you nurture that child. Always address their positive traits before offering criticism. A little encouragement and reassurance will make all the difference in the world for this double-1 energy.

▪ THE MISUNDERSTOOD 8 ▪

The nineteen years I have been a practicing Numerologist, there is one number that often writes to me in dismay or hurt, or seems the victim. It is the number 8. I recently received *seven letters in a row* from 8 Life Path men and women who were in pain, and that is what has prompted me to write about it.

Here are three of them: The first letter was from an 8 asking for help with the daughter she was about to disown; the second wrote that she and her husband had no money and their relationship in general was not working; a third stated that he had never been successful in love or business. In each one of these letters, I discerned an 8 pattern, even before I checked the actual dates. Every one of them was either an 8 Life Path, was born on an 8 Birth Day day, or had an 8 Attitude.

When an 8 is in your birth numbers it is a significant part of you. It is a vibration you must find a way to master. I would say to an 8, get a piece of paper and trace the number 8 and realize that you are often doing in life what the numeral does on the paper. The number 8 looks like the symbol of infinity, which goes around and around forever. There are times when the 8s feel like they are going crazy, because they too feel as though they are going around and around forever. The 8 must really keep this in mind.

MARTHA STEWART: A CASE STUDY OF THE 8

Martha Stewart was born an 8 Life Path. As a child, her family had very little. A lack of money is intolerable for the 8 Life Path, even at a very young age. Early on Martha was showing signs of her future entrepreneurship, baking pies and cakes and developing a respect for the art of cooking.

After her difficult divorce, Martha threw herself into her catering company, which, after many years and a great deal of hard work, became Martha Stewart Omnimedia. Thanks to an unparalleled drive, intelligence, and savvy business sense, Martha Stewart made herself into a household name.

No matter how successful Martha became, her early childhood memories haunted her as someone who would never have enough. Martha's stock was worth a billion dollars, but inside she still felt it was not enough. In Kahlil Gibran's *The Prophet* we are asked: "Is not dread of thirst when your well is full, a thirst that is unquenchable?" That was exactly what was happening with Martha. No matter how successful, she was afraid that she didn't have enough. This was not greed, as many might think, but fear. When Martha Stewart made the decision to sell approximately 4,000 shares of her ImClone stock—just a drop in the bucket of her multimillion-dollar empire—she was acting on the 8 impulse to maintain financial control. That one action had disastrous results in her life. Her stock price has fallen; she's had to step down as the CEO of the company that bears her name; and comedians across the land are milking the "how will she decorate her jail cell?" punch line for all it's worth. I don't laugh because I see in her numbers how this happened and I have empathy for her. I truly hope that she will be able to find her way.

I would also ask the 8 to be more open-minded about the definition of an 8 Life Path. The 8 is here to establish financial security, but that does not mean that you are materialistic and greedy. It simply means that more than any other number, you are miserable if you cannot pay the bills, take care of yourself, and have economic protection. Money is a part of life. If you use your natural gifts, the income will follow.

There are two types of 8s, by the way. Some of them think that having money is their security, and they put every cent in the bank; the other 8s let everything they make slip right through their fingers, because they are extravagant givers. An 8 must find a balance between miserly hoarding and foolish spending. Numerology is here to help you work through the challenges of your particular energy or vibration. Nothing in what I share here should make an 8 feel put down, or less than any other number, because you aren't.

There are many enormously successful and admired people who are 8 Life Paths. One of them is Paul Newman, who started a line of healthy, organic foods whose profits go to charitable endeavors. Newman is a double 8—he was born on an 8 Birth Day and has an 8 Life Path. Other thriving 8 Life Paths are Barbra Streisand, Diane Sawyer, Matt Damon, and Sandra Bullock.

I want you 8s to continue to strive for your goals, financial and personal. Learn to choose your words carefully, so that you don't unintentionally offend the people in your lives. If you have over the years adopted the role of victim, work on ending it now. Go over the affirmations for your vibration in chapter 4. Say the words until they become part of you. If a negative situation does arise, be accountable. Look for whatever role you may have played in the scenario. The minute we look for others to blame for our situations in life is the minute we lose our own power.

When you are raised in poverty, however, and you have not reprogrammed your mind, then you'll always feel like you have no money. I know, both as a Numerologist and life counselor, if you don't change the way you think about money, no matter how much you make, you will find yourself going broke over and over.

MONEY ? EVIL

Often clients with money issues back up their experiences with this quote: "Money is the root of all evil." But did you know that's not the real quotation? The correct quote is: "*The love of* money is the root of all evil." When an 8 Life Path is living on the positive side of the energy, they don't love *or* hate money—they feel in control of their finances, and thus have no need to attach emotions to the concept of money.

God put us on a planet that costs money, so I believe He must also have a plan to help us *make* money. I find there are various people, no matter what their Life Path Number, who feel somewhat guilty about wanting extra money. I put it to them this way: If you were a millionaire, wouldn't you want to take care of the people in your life? Money gives you the power to help yourself and others. That is when it starts to make sense to them.

Whether we have an 8 in our chart or not, our feelings about money often get bred into us as children. This is why people who win the lottery often go broke after just a couple of years. Deep down, they don't really believe the money is theirs, so they have trouble holding on to it. We all need to reprogram our minds so we see that money is the means to an end—not an end in itself.

For anyone who has money problems, I would suggest a rigid adherence to a program of affirmations of plenty. Here are two excellent affirmations for the Life Path 8, and anyone with financial issues:

Affirmation 1:

I believe in infinite abundance and the money is always there.

Affirmation 2:

I am open to receiving the bounty of this generous universe.

The more I give, the more I receive.

It takes just fifteen to twenty minutes a day to erase the inner tapes of negativity that we so often carry around in our psyches. The only real reason we are here on this planet is to establish inner peace, love others, and make this world a better place. That should be the ultimate goal.

▪ MISSING NUMBERS ▪

People often say to me, "Which are my best numbers—the ones I get along with . . . and don't?" The truth is, every single number is in us, or should be. When you break down your birth certificate name and your date of birth, you should be able to find a 1 in there, a 2 in there, a 4. If there is a number missing, study those particular numbers' traits, and be aware of that quality that is lacking in you. If you're missing a 2, maybe you need to be more feeling with people. If you are missing a 3, you need to be more of a communicator.

According to Numerology, in order to be truly happy, you should embrace every number. That is the only way we will ever be able to coexist peacefully. You should understand the positive and negative of every number, starting with your own personal chart.

The placement of the number in your chart shows its significance. If it's your Life Path, it's your most important number. If it's your Destiny Number, it's about fulfilling your destiny. If it's your Birth Day Number, it is what people get as their first impression of you. If it's your Attitude Number, it's what you're projecting. That's why you want to study each number 1 through 9.

Note: If you find you are missing a number, locate and read about it in chapter 3. Be aware of what the number represents and try to implement the positive attributes of the number in your life.

Twenty

Using the Numbers to Attract Positive Energies

As we've already discussed in the affirmations chapter, sometimes it takes just the smallest effort on your part to attract new, more positive energies into your life. The same goes for numbers. By surrounding yourself with the numbers that attract the vibrations your life is missing, you can actually change your circumstances for the better. Whatever you desire—be it money, love, or security—can be yours.

Perhaps the most important way you can attract a different energy is by bringing numbers into your home. The way to do it is to post the numbers whose energies you want to attract in the room where the energy belongs. A bedroom door is a good place to put a 2, to encourage love. Have fun and be creative! My clients are forever telling me how the numbers they've brought into their lives have changed their life for the better. Let's look at two of my favorite examples.

▪ THE FRIENDLY 3 ▪

Recently, I received a letter from a woman named Peggy telling me how the use of numbers had changed her sister's life. Her sister, Lisa, went off to college and was living in the dorms. She felt very alone and had no friends on the college campus. After hearing me on the radio and picking up my book, she put the number 3 on the wall of her dorm room. Within a few weeks, she started making friends right and left. Now her dorm room is the place where everyone wants to hang out. She actually has to find ways to get them to go back to their own rooms! Peggy was thanking me for simplifying Numerology in such a way that Lisa could use it to make her college experience a much better one. By giving her dorm room the number 3, Lisa was able to solve her loneliness problem.

▪ SHOW ME THE MONEY ▪

I got a letter from one of my clients, Cindy, who told me that she had changed the address of her home. She lived in a house of 7, which is the house of study. But money was something she needed more of, so she added a 1 on the inside of her door (7 + 1 = 8) to create an 8 vibration home. Within one year, her husband had almost tripled his income!

What's more, studying the numbers made her realize she wanted to find a way to use her creative energies. She answered an ad to do voiceover work and got hired to do radio commercials at a local station. Now not only was she feeling creatively fulfilled, she was bringing more money into the house as well.

Cindy isn't the only person who has used the number 8 for financial success. Mark and Jo Anne decided to try an experiment. Mark owned a construction company and business had been very slow. In an effort to try to bring more financial wealth into their lives, they posted the number 8 on the wall in the home office where they write all of their bills. Within a week of putting up the number 8, the husband landed three different jobs!

Another client of mine found he was always flat broke for several days before his next paycheck was due. He decided to give the money number a try, and put a piece of paper with an 8 on it in his wallet. He wrote me a letter to say that ever since then, he has had extra money in his wallet on the day his new paycheck arrives.

I love hearing these stories of how the use of the number 8 can plant the seeds of prosperity in your life. The fact that the 3 can attract more people into your life when you are feeling lonely, and that love can come right to your door because of the 2. Here's to the power of numbers! They never cease to amaze me.

Twenty-one

A Numerologist's Philosophy for Living

Numerology is more than a career for me, it's a way of life. As a spiritual person, I have always had a strong belief in God and seen meaning in the world every day. But until I discovered the science of numbers, I didn't have a concrete way to share my vision with others. I believe God brought Numerology into my life so that I would be able to help guide others in this world, and help heal them from the wounds that are a part of life.

Seeing so many people find hope and understanding through the numbers has only reaffirmed my faith in their power. I hope that through this book, I've been able to give you a glimpse of some of the amazing stories I encounter every day through my readings. I want to share a couple of stories that remind me that "today is all we have. Tomorrow may never come."

▪ JOHN F. KENNEDY JR. ▪
59577, Attitude 9

John F. Kennedy Jr. was handsome, healthy, and wealthy beyond most people's dreams. His life, however, was not an easy one. He stays in our national consciousness as a brave three-year-old boy saluting his father's casket. Despite the worldwide exposure and concern, he was still just a little child who had lost his father. His beloved uncle Robert took over as a father figure, but soon he too was lost—once again suddenly and through violence.

John's mother married Aristotle Onassis, in part to protect her children from violence in America, and John has been quoted as saying that Onassis was a true father to him. His mother liked Onassis less well, and the marriage quickly dissolved. Once again John had lost someone crucial to him. He had a series of well-publicized romances and finally seemed to have found love with Carolyn Bessette. The magazine *George* was floundering, but there was a new movement to get Kennedy into politics. He seemed to be warming to the idea, and few doubted that if he decided to, he would be a successful candidate for any office—even President. He was adored as America's crown prince.

John had repeating numbers 5 and 7 in his personal chart. These numbers are all about staying busy and to just keep moving. John's passion for in-line skating, biking, jogging in Central Park, and flying his plane confirms he was definitely living his life by the numbers. Even on the hazy night he went flying to Martha's Vineyard, that same day he had a cast removed from a broken ankle caused by a poor landing of his Buckeye-powered parachute six weeks earlier. The 5s and 7s in his chart would promote this "never a dull moment" behavior.

Then suddenly and without warning he was gone. Youth, health, fame went with him. You can bet that John had no idea his time on this planet was up. His untimely death reminds us that there's only one real gift that we have in this lifetime: the gift of life itself.

■ SARAH'S STORY ■

Sarah was a client who told me after her first reading that she had gotten more from Numerology in an hour than she had in three years of counseling.

We continued working together for several days. I found among her male suitors someone who had five numbers out of five with her, so she was excited about looking into that relationship.

Sarah was a moving force in her community and had a prestigious job in the public sector. She was pregnant by a man who had left her, and was the mother of a two-year-old girl and a four-year-old boy. Empowered by what she had learned in her Numerology sessions, she had decided to have the baby, even though the father had left her, because she had the strength to do it.

Over the next several days I started getting calls from Sarah's friends asking for readings. I've never known anyone, even a celebrity, with a following like Sarah's. She called me again and told me how amazing it all was for her, that Numerology made perfect sense. She had read the books I had recommended and was so happy.

Two weeks after first talking with Sarah, I got another call—from a man who loved her. He started sobbing and told me she had died in a car crash. There was no way I could believe it. I called her office and it was true. She had died in a car crash the night before.

Few things in my life have shaken me like this. "How could this bright light be extinguished so soon?" I was crying and asked out loud, "God, why did this happen?" The message came to me in a clear voice: "Today is all you've got. If you're not in the job you want to be in, get out. If you are in an abusive situation, get out. Today is your future. When you worry about the distant future and what it's going to be, you're not really living today." I was glad Sarah had taken hold of her destiny before her life ended, and I encourage you to use the information in this book to improve your life today. After all, it's all you've got.

"You are the Master of each moment of your life."

—Yogananda

• FINAL THOUGHTS •

The Gift of Numerology: There's No Such Thing as a Stranger

When you study the science of Numerology, you really will start to see the patterns in everything and everyone—even in someone who is a perfect stranger. One morning when I was at the post office, a beautiful older woman walked in wearing an electric blue sweater covered with sparkling beads. She also had on blue pants to match, blue shoes, short elegantly coiffed hair, perfect makeup, and a truly engaging smile. The woman looked like the very personification of the celebration of life—a 5 if ever I had seen one. I figured she must be born on a 5 day.

She sat down next to me and we made small talk about the crowd in the post office. When I looked into her gentle blue eyes, I could see her kind spirit, and I was sure that she must have a number 2 in her chart as well. I finally told her that I was a Numerologist and that I would love to know her birth date. She was born 6/5/1922. Let's break down her birth numbers. She was born on the 5th day, that would give her a 5 Birth Day Number. Her Attitude Number, which comes from adding the month and day $6 + 5 = 11 = 1 + 1 = 2$, gave her a 2 Attitude. To find her Life Path, I added all of her birth numbers together ($6 + 5 + 1 + 9 + 2 + 2 = 16 = 1 + 6 = 7$) and found that she was a 7 Life Path. So I was right! She looked like a 5 because her Birth Day number was a 5. This explained her joyous appearance; the kindness that was emanating from her came from her 2 Attitude. I began to tell her what her numbers meant, and her face lit up. She further validated the numbers by telling me that she stayed young by taking dance classes every weekday. What a perfect physical and emotional outlet for a 5 Birth Day. She also said her family nicknamed her Pollyanna because she always had an optimistic attitude.

"Optimistic" would certainly be an apt word to describe the 2 Attitude Number. She was delighted with my accuracy. Since she had a 7 Life Path, I asked her about her spirituality and she said she had spent a lifetime seeking answers to the eternal questions. I told her that if she would give me her phone number, I would keep her updated on my speaking engagements. She looked at me rather nervously and said, "I don't give out my phone number. Who did you say you were again?"

I could have fallen down laughing. Her 7 Life Path's need for privacy had reared its suspicious head. She gave me her PO box number and said that I was welcome to keep in touch with her that way. Talk about a case study of Numerology. This woman and I had never met before, yet by knowing her numbers, I knew her completely. If it were not for the science of Numerology, I could very easily have been hurt when she pulled back and refused to give me her phone number. Instead, I had complete understanding and her actions made perfect sense. *I say there is no such thing as a stranger when you've got their numbers.* This wonderful woman reminded me of how true that statement really is. As you continue to play with these numbers, pay attention. As you come to know each person better, even if their numbers are Toxic to you, you will understand where they're coming from instead of taking it personally. The insight on each vibration can bring about more peace in our lives, which I believe is what we all really seeking. Learn the information in this book and you will never see life the same way again. Numerology is truly a gift for all of us. All we have to do is apply this remarkable knowledge in our day-to-day lives.

APPENDIX A: Celebrity Life Path Numbers

NAME	BIRTH DATE	LIFE PATH #
Buster Keaton	10/4/1895	1
David Letterman	4/12/1947	1
Drew Barrymore	2/22/1975	1
Jack Nicholson	4/22/1937	1
James Taylor	3/12/1948	1
Jerry Lewis	3/16/1926	1
Lou Diamond Phillips	2/17/1962	1
Nicolas Cage	1/7/1964	1
Ralph Lauren	10/14/1939	1
Raquel Welch	9/5/1940	1
Rita Hayworth	10/17/1918	1
Sammy Davis Jr.	12/08/1925	1
Steve Guttenberg	8/24/1958	1
Sting	10/2/1951	1
Suzanne Somers	10/16/1946	1
Billy Crystal	3/14/1947	2
Diana Ross	3/26/1944	2
Frank Zappa	12/21/1940	2
Henry Kissinger	5/27/1923	2
Jack Benny	2/14/1894	2
Jane Wyman	1/4/1914	2
Jay Leno	4/28/1950	2
Kim Basinger	12/8/1953	2
Madonna	8/16/1958	2
Marie Osmond	10/13/1959	2

NAME	BIRTH DATE	LIFE PATH #
Sidney Poitier	2/20/1924	2
Alan Alda	1/28/1936	3
Ann Landers	7/4/1918	3
Barbara Walters	9/25/1931	3
Bert Parks	12/30/1914	3
Charlton Heston	10/4/1924	3
Connie Chung	8/20/1946	3
David Bowie	1/8/1947	3
Faye Dunaway	1/14/1941	3
Gore Vidal	10/3/1925	3
Groucho Marx	10/2/1890	3
Kevin Costner	1/18/1955	3
Lloyd Bridges	1/15/1913	3
Michele Lee	6/24/1942	3
River Phoenix	8/23/1970	3
Tracey Ullman	12/30/1959	3
Arnold Schwarzenegger	7/30/1947	4
Brad Pitt	12/18/1963	4
Dolly Parton	1/19/1946	4
Elton John	3/25/1947	4
J. D. Salinger	1/1/1919	4
James A. Michener	2/3/1907	4
Julia Louis-Dreyfus	1/13/1961	4
Karl Lagerfeld	9/10/1938	4
Keanu Reeves	9/2/1964	4
Kim Novak	2/13/1933	4
LeVar Burton	2/16/1957	4
Luciano Pavarotti	10/12/1935	4
Maury Povich	1/17/1939	4
Nat "King" Cole	3/17/1919	4
Olympia Dukakis	6/20/1931	4
Sarah Ferguson	10/15/1959	4
Sarah Jessica Parker	3/25/1965	4
Will Smith	9/25/1968	4
Ava Gardner	12/24/1922	5
Bob Mackie	3/24/1940	5
Denzel Washington	12/28/1954	5
Desi Arnaz	3/2/1917	5
Gloria Estefan	9/1/1957	5

NAME	BIRTH DATE	LIFE PATH #
Howard Stern	1/12/1954	5
Lee Iacocca	10/15/1924	5
Lily Tomlin	9/1/1939	5
Marlene Dietrich	12/27/1901	5
Meg Tilly	2/14/1960	5
Michael J. Fox	6/9/1961	5
Ron Howard	3/1/1954	5
Sigourney Weaver	10/8/1949	5
Steve Martin	8/14/1945	5
Walter Matthau	10/1/1920	5
Charlie Sheen	9/3/1965	6
Christopher Reeve	9/25/1952	6
Danny Kaye	1/18/1913	6
Fred Astaire	5/10/1899	6
Heather Locklear	9/25/1961	6
Howard Hughes	12/24/1905	6
Humphrey Bogart	1/23/1899	6
Ira Gershwin	12/6/1896	6
J.R.R. Tolkien	1/3/1892	6
Jimmy Durante	2/10/1893	6
John Lennon	10/9/1940	6
Matthew Broderick	3/21/1962	6
Michael Jackson	8/29/1958	6
Phil Donahue	12/21/1935	6
Rosie O'Donnell	3/21/1962	6
Stephen King	9/21/1947	6
Ted Koppel	2/8/1940	6
T.S. Eliot	9/26/1888	6
Angela Lansbury	10/16/1925	7
Cesar Romero	2/15/1907	7
Donna Karan	10/2/1948	7
Donny Osmond	12/9/1957	7
Emily Dickinson	12/10/1830	7
Harry Connick Jr.	9/11/1967	7
Helen Gurley Brown	2/18/1922	7
Hugh Grant	9/9/1960	7
Jerry Seinfeld	4/29/1954	7
Joseph Wambaugh	1/22/1937	7
Kiefer Sutherland	12/18/1966	7

NAME	BIRTH DATE	LIFE PATH #
Michael Keaton	9/9/1951	7
Muhammad Ali	1/17/1942	7
Roger Moore	10/14/1927	7
Susan Sarandon	10/4/1946	7
Tennessee Ernie Ford	2/13/1919	8
Andy Rooney	1/14/1919	8
Aretha Franklin	3/25/1942	8
Cindy Crawford	2/20/1966	8
Corbin Bernsen	9/7/1954	8
Diane Keaton	1/5/1946	8
Diane Sawyer	12/22/1945	8
Geena Davis	1/21/1957	8
Lucille Ball	8/6/1911	8
Marlee Matlin	8/24/1965	8
Michael Eisner	3/7/1942	8
Pope John Paul II	5/18/1920	8
Bette Davis	4/5/1908	9
Bill Murray	9/21/1950	9
Elvis Aron Presley	1/8/1935	9
George Burns	1/20/1896	9
Gilda Radner	6/28/1946	9
Jane Curtin	9/6/1947	9
Jim Carrey	1/17/1962	9
Ray Charles	9/23/1930	9
Shelley Long	8/23/1949	9
Tyra Banks	12/4/1973	9

NAME	BIRTH DATE	ATTITUDE #
Aretha Franklin	3/25	1
Gary Coleman	2/8	1
Gloria Steinem	3/25	1
Howard Cosell	3/25	1
Jack Lemmon	2/8	1
James Dean	2/8	1
John Grisham	2/8	1
Lana Turner	2/8	1
Mary Steenburgen	2/8	1
Nick Nolte	2/8	1
Paul Michael Glaser	3/25	1

NAME	BIRTH DATE	ATTITUDE #
Sarah Jessica Parker	3/25	1
Ted Koppel	2/8	1
Alan Alda	1/28	2
Cybill Shepherd	2/18	2
Jim Croce	1/10	2
Joe Pesci	2/9	2
John Travolta	2/18	2
Pat Benatar	1/10	2
Rod Stewart	1/10	2
Yoko Ono	2/18	2
Beau Bridges	12/9	3
Buck Henry	12/9	3
Cuba Gooding Jr.	1/2	3
Dick Van Patten	12/9	3
Donny Osmond	12/9	3
Douglas Fairbanks, Jr.	12/9	3
Jim Bakker	1/2	3
John Malkovich	12/9	3
Kirk Douglas	12/9	3
Naomi Judd	1/11	3
Redd Foxx	12/9	3
Carly Simon	6/25	4
Charlene Tilton	12/1	4
Dick Martin	1/30	4
George Michael	6/25	4
Howard Stern	1/12	4
Hugh Hefner	4/9	4
Kirstie Alley	1/12	4
Mel Gibson	1/3	4
Richard Pryor	12/1	4
Victoria Principal	1/3	4
Billy Idol	11/30	5
Chris Issak	6/26	5
Dick Clark	11/30	5
Dyan Cannon	1/4	5
Jane Wyman	1/4	5
Julia Louis-Dreyfus	1/13	5
Mark Twain	11/30	5
Mary Martin	11/30	5

NAME	BIRTH DATE	ATTITUDE #
Spike Lee	3/20	5
Pearl Bailey	3/29	5
Alice Cooper	2/4	6
Andy Rooney	1/14	6
Clint Black	2/4	6
David Brenner	2/4	6
Diane Keaton	1/5	6
Faye Dunaway	1/14	6
Helen Keller	6/27	6
Kim Novak	2/13	6
Robert Duvall	1/5	6
Stockard Channing	2/13	6
Barbara Hershey	2/5	7
Bonnie Franklin	1/6	7
Charo	1/15	7
Danny Thomas	1/6	7
Gilda Radner	6/28	7
John Cusack	6/28	7
Kathy Bates	6/28	7
Loretta Young	1/6	7
Mel Brooks	6/28	7
Red Buttons	2/5	7
Cyndi Lauper	6/20	8
Dan Aykroyd	7/1	8
Danny Aiello	6/20	8
Deborah Harry	7/1	8
Errol Flynn	6/20	8
Jamie Farr	7/1	8
John Goodman	6/20	8
Katie Couric	1/7	8
Kenny Loggins	1/7	8
Lionel Richie	6/20	8
Martin Landau	6/20	8
Nicolas Cage	1/7	8
Nicole Kidman	6/20	8
Olivia de Havilland	7/1	8
Olympia Dukakis	6/20	8
Pamela Anderson	7/1	8
Princess Diana	7/1	8

NAME	BIRTH DATE	ATTITUDE #
Andy Kaufman	1/17	9
Elvis Aron Presley	1/8	9
Evel Knievel	10/17	9
Jane Russell	6/21	9
Juliette Lewis	6/21	9
Lena Horne	6/30	9
LeVar Burton	2/16	9
Meredith Baxter	6/21	9
Rona Barrett	10/8	9
Soupy Sales	1/8	9

APPENDIX B: Suggested Reading

Getting to "I Do" by Dr. Patricia Allen
The Choice by Og Mandino
Resolving Conflict Sooner by Kare Anderson
The Healing of Emotion by Chris Griscom
The One Minute Millionaire by Mark Victor Hansen and Robert G. Allen
The Prophet by Kahlil Gibran
Where There Is Light by Paramahansa Yogananda
Wishcraft by Barbara Sher

APPENDIX C: Bibliography

Barrat, Rodford. *The Elements of Numerology*. Great Britain: Element Books, 1994.

Bishop, Barbara J. *Numerology: Universal Vibrations of Numbers*. St. Paul, MN: Llewellyn Worldwide, 1990.

Connolly, Eileen. *The Connolly Book of Numbers*. North Hollywood, CA: Newcastle Publishing Co., 1988.

Cooper, D. Jason. *Understanding Numerology*. Wellingborough, UK: IHEA Guarian Press, 1986.

Dodge, Ellin. *Numerology Has Your Number*. New York: Simon & Schuster, 1988.

Gawain, Shakti. *Creative Visualization*. Novato: New World Library, 2002.

Gendlin, Eugene T. *Focusing*. New York: Bantam Publishing, 1981.

Goodwin, Matthew O. *Numerology: The Complete Guide*. North Hollywood: Newcastle Publishing, 1981.

Hay, Louise L. *You Can Heal Your Life*. Carlsbad, CA: Hay House Publishing.

Line, Julia. *The Numerology Workbook*. New York: Sterling Publishing, 1985.

Linn, Denise D. *Sacred Space*. Canada: Wellspring/Ballantine Books, 1995.

Ruiz, Don Miguel *The Four Agreements*. San Rafael: Amber-Allen Publishing, 1997.

If you would like more information on getting a personal reading, more books and tapes, or dates for a workshop with Glynis McCants, write for a pamphlet:

ADDRESS: Glynis Has Your Number
           PO Box 81057
           San Marino, CA 91118-1057

E-MAIL: numbersladyinfo@aol.com

OFFICE: 1-877-686-2373
FAX: (626) 614-9292

Our website address is www.numberslady.com.
The e-mail address is GlynisMcC@aol.com.